"Powerful and practical—in business, too. Shore's six-step process seamlessly integrates advanced research with straightforward advice. By *Setting Boundaries That Stick*, leaders and managers maintain honest, genuine relationships with the same subordinates they must sometimes disappoint. Every executive and management team in my firm's twenty-year client history would benefit from this groundbreaking book."

—**Ed Muzio**, best-selling author of *Iterate*; and cocreator of the
industry's only real-time, simultaneous executive team
behavioral intervention

"What a gift! This book is full of practices you can use to change your relationship with yourself and with others. In these pages, you will find the complexity of the brain and boundary work illuminated in a way you can understand and apply in your real life to move forward in your healing journey. It's practical, heartfelt, and beautifully written."

—**Jessica Baum, LMHC**, psychotherapist, coach, and author of
Anxiously Attached

"*Setting Boundaries That Stick* is a trusted guide for anyone who has ever felt challenged to set personal boundaries in a truly relational way. Based on the latest cutting-edge neuroscience, yet preeminently practical, Juliane Shore has written a heartfelt book that teaches all of us how to speak our truths with empowering integrity. This book is destined to be a classic for therapists and clients alike."

—**Gary D. Salyer, PhD**, transformational relationship mentor,
and author of *Safe to Love Again*

"*Setting Boundaries That Stick* is a standalone guide for individuals who are looking to grow in their personal lives and feel more secure in their relationships, as well as therapists who will discover this book to be a clear and compassionate masterpiece that will complement their work with clients. Juliane's approach through a trauma-informed lens brings richness and meaning to the essential work of setting boundaries. Case examples are well crafted, practical, and relatable. I highly recommend this life-changing book that you will run to share with your support system."

—**Jennifer Udler, LCSW-C**, author of *Walk and Talk Therapy*

"As a somatic trauma therapist, this is the book I've been waiting for! Using examples based in relational neuroscience, Jules teaches the reader to identify and express the boundaries needed to feel secure. I love her empowering, compassionate, non-shaming approach to setting boundaries, a subject many of us find confusing. I highly recommend this book to anyone who wants to learn to express and hold boundaries from an embodied place."

—**Laura Reagan, LCSW-C**, host of the *Therapy Chat* podcast, and founder of the Trauma Therapist Network

"*Setting Boundaries That Stick* offers the most comprehensive, sophisticated, and scientifically rigorous exploration of boundaries that I have ever come across, all while managing to be incredibly readable and practical. Through accessible descriptions of neuroscience, clearly outlined steps, and exercises to help you along the way, this book is sure to change your relationship with yourself, your world, and your loved ones."

—**Tori Olds, PhD**, cofounder of Deep Eddy Psychotherapy, and associate instructor at the Coherence Therapy Institute

"Juliane Taylor Shore is a brilliant and trusted guide for rafting the rivers of intimate relationships, pointing out boulders to avoid, and modeling how to paddle through the rapids with strength and grace. She lives what she teaches, and her recommendations in *Setting Boundaries That Stick* are pragmatic and inspiring. Shore's deep intuition and fun writing style make reading and practicing the steps in this book a joyful, full-bodied treat!"

—**Gena St. David, PhD**, professor of counselor
education at Seminary of the Southwest, and author
of *The Brain and the Spirit*

"*Setting Boundaries That Stick* was profoundly helpful for me personally and professionally. As a licensed marriage and family therapist, teaching people how to set healthy boundaries is an essential part of the work. Juliane Taylor Shore does an amazing job articulating how to value yourself and others, and have the confidence to set boundaries in every relationship. She has been a great teacher to me."

—**Shane Birkel, LMFT**, host of the *Couples
Therapist Couch* podcast

SETTING BOUNDARIES THAT STICK

How Neurobiology Can Help You
Rewire Your Brain to Feel Safe,
Connected, and Empowered

JULIANE TAYLOR SHORE, LMFT

New Harbinger Publications, Inc.

Publisher's Note

This publication is designed to provide accurate and authoritative information in regard to the subject matter covered. It is sold with the understanding that the publisher is not engaged in rendering psychological, financial, legal, or other professional services. If expert assistance or counseling is needed, the services of a competent professional should be sought.

NEW HARBINGER PUBLICATIONS is a registered trademark of New Harbinger Publications, Inc.

New Harbinger Publications is an employee-owned company.

Copyright © 2023 by Juliane Taylor Shore
New Harbinger Publications, Inc.
5720 Shattuck Avenue
Oakland, CA 94609
www.newharbinger.com

Cover design by Amy Shoup

Acquired by Jennye Garibaldi

Edited by Marisa Solis

Library of Congress Cataloging-in-Publication Data on file

FSC
www.fsc.org
MIX
Paper from
responsible sources
FSC® C011935

Printed in the United States of America

25   24   23

10   9   8   7   6   5   4   3   2   1   First Printing

For Stella and Adam

Contents

Foreword   vii

Introduction   1

Chapter 1   Boundaries and Your Brain   5

Chapter 2   Six Steps to Setting an External Boundary   23

Chapter 3   Psychological Boundaries   45

Chapter 4   Containing Boundaries   71

Chapter 5   Physical Boundaries   89

Chapter 6   Using All Your Boundary Skills Together   109

Chapter 7   Setting Boundaries with Yourself   119

Chapter 8   Boundaries and Openness in Close Relationships   133

Chapter 9   Clear Is Kind   143

Acknowledgments   155

References   158

Foreword

I've been practicing as a psychotherapist for twenty years, and I've been on my own healing journey even longer. All these years that I've been teaching people how to relationship better, I've also been learning alongside them: healing my own broken parts, repairing my relational wounds, and, together with my partner, breaking intergenerational patterns in the hopes of passing forward as much healing as we can, so our children may benefit from the footing we gain.

For the past several years, Juliane Taylor Shore and I have been cofacilitating relationship workshops and cohosting the *Why Does My Partner* podcast. Over this time, she's become a cherished colleague and mentor. When Jules invited me to write this foreword, I didn't fully recognize the ways agreeing to this process would open me to new and deeper learnings. As I read *Setting Boundaries That Stick,* on a felt-sense level I better understood what boundaries really are, why they're tough to implement well, and how healthy boundaries help us to more fully come back into connection with our own integrity and wisdom.

Healthy boundaries are conscious practices *we* do; they are not what others do or don't do. Healthy boundaries will help you to navigate hard relational moments. They will help you to align with your own intentions. They will help you to act in congruence with your own values. They will help you to experience pride in your own behavior rather than confusion or distress. They will help you to trust in yourself, even (and especially) when things are hard. And navigating this world can be hard.

Where did you learn how to navigate hard relational moments? My earliest learnings centered around protecting myself from the reactive, inflexible, and defensive behaviors modeled by my parents after having been passed down to them through generational lines: walling off, shutting out, attempts to manipulate, dominate, control, or deny others' reality. As a young person, I often felt confused and powerless. And then, like others had been with me, I attempted to get people to treat me in ways that would make me feel better: through volatility, manipulation, anger, withdrawal... the list goes on (and I am sure you can add to it yourself).

The skill of watching your own mind and noticing the automated, unconscious, reactive strategies you formed as historically protective responses will help you better meet hard relational moments with vulnerability and courage. Gently making space to witness your patterns will help guide you toward greater rootedness, clarity, and authenticity.

In the pages of this book, you will see yourself. At times you may feel some remorse; I did. When I read passages aloud to my partner, we felt remorse together. Those moments both humbled us and presented a gift. Remorse points us back home to our integrity; it makes it easier for us to get unstuck and to find a different way forward. It's the avoiding of remorse, grief, discord, dread, of not wanting things to not feel good, that keeps us stuck. The brain-savvy boundary practices you're about to discover in this book will help you to *be with*, rather than avoid, these hard feelings.

In its pages you will also find a compassion, understanding, and acceptance that is incredibly necessary. As you begin to digest the skills offered, templates to participate in creating a more just world, they will hold you. This practice begins with owning the power of your influence and aligning your actions and words with your behaviors and values. Compassion makes boundaries work. It shifts the focus; it shifts everything. And learning to engage your own compassion in this work will move you from reactionary to revolutionary. It's deeply personal and profoundly relational, and it holds the power to change the world, starting with you.

The practices presented build upon one another and are themselves built upon the mechanics of how our brains work. As you apply them, they'll help you feel safe, connected, and empowered; you'll learn to make better sense of yourself. In moments of discord, you might find you can discern your truth without diminishing another's in an unconscious attempt to defend yourself. Empowerment lies in your ability to respond; in the shift from unconscious, autopilot reactivity toward conscious responsiveness. As you develop a practice of pausing between what you are thinking and feeling and what you are speaking and doing, you'll begin to undo aloneness and believe in your growing capacity to navigate hard moments and enjoy easeful flows in all of your relationships.

I've been implementing these practices in my life and relationships and in my work with clients. While Jules's teachings challenge my clients and me to engage with hard stuff, they do so in a way that simultaneously opens new possibilities and offers deeply profound relief.

I wish you the same.

—Rebecca Wong, LCSW-R

Introduction

You may have opened this book because you want to trust yourself and feel empowered in more areas of your life. You may have picked it up because it seems hard to feel deeply connected to other people and truly honor your own needs at the same time. You may want to learn how to respond to others from your best self, rather than just react at the mercy of others' behavior. To experience life fully, you probably already know that a working set of boundaries will help. Welcome.

No matter what kind of struggles you've had in the past, this book and the tools it offers will help you discover, create, communicate, and hold your boundaries. At the end of this book, I want you to close it knowing you now have a clear map for upholding your boundaries in most situations that life brings you. You will have begun the inner work necessary to follow that map all the way through, every time. I'm glad you've decided to transform your boundaries so that you can trust yourself, have safer connections with others, and, ultimately, live a joyful life.

To set boundaries that stick, learning to work *with* your brain is essential. The strategies I'll share utilize discoveries in neurobiology and how our brains and bodies work in relationships. I found these strategies because I needed them in my own life and needed to help my clients work more effectively with their own boundaries and brains, too.

I got into studying neurobiology at the beginning of my training to become a therapist. I was making a career change: I'd been working in auto repairs, turning wrenches for a living. When I looked at my graduate school curriculum, I noticed that there were no classes on the workings of the brain. It struck me as odd that we were trying to help people develop greater mental health but were not being given any information about the brain or the nature of the mind. Personally, I wouldn't try to repair a brake system without a solid understanding of how a brake system worked!

This gap in my education started my quest to learn about the brain. That journey has led me to weave interpersonal neurobiology into all I do, to integrate the discoveries into my practice, and to teach other clinicians how to do the same. Over the last fifteen years of working as a therapist, I have served nearly a thousand clients from many kinds of backgrounds and have taught healers from all over the world. Each of these people has benefited from knowing more about how our brains work in relationships and how to feel safer while honoring their own needs.

I am a white, cisgender woman in a heterosexual relationship, raised in the Western culture of the United States. This imparts a great deal of privilege to me, which I strive to use with care and solidarity. I have heard lots of folks talk about boundaries in an advice-giving sort of way, often from the point of view of a culture and worldview that is Western, individualistic, and grounded in personal growth. I view boundaries differently. I think about them from the perspective of how a person—in any culture and any environment—stays feeling safer. I am holding awareness that feeling safer is easier in some bodies than in others because of the pervasiveness of societal oppressions. Asserting boundaries is easier or harder depending on what body you are in and who is around you. I want your boundaries to be yours and fit just right for you, no matter your background or social location. This means that every tool I offer should be adapted to fit your life and circumstances, and I want you to use these ideas while trusting yourself and your wisdom. I invite you to use these tools to get more in touch with your own wisdom and to trust yourself more than you do right now.

I know I have no idea what boundaries might be just right for a person from a close-knit family from a collectivist culture or what boundaries are the right form of resistance for a person who is the target of marginalization or what boundaries are right for you in your spot in the world with your marriage or with your kids or colleagues or friends. I do not believe other people's boundaries are for me to define, and I do not believe there are right boundaries or wrong boundaries, good boundaries or bad boundaries. These pages instead will give you tools to work with your brain to discover for yourself what boundaries feel right for you and when you want them to be more firm or more flexible. These tools are about serving you and your boundary needs, no matter who or where you are.

Many of us are taught to navigate relationships with the feeling that protecting ourselves will somehow hurt other people—that we must choose between either being hurt or hurting someone else—but this is simply not true. I cannot think of a single client or student who has not benefited from rethinking how boundaries work and practicing new ways of setting them. I hope it will help you, too.

In this book, I introduce a six-step process for setting boundaries. When you start to experiment with the steps, you may find your own areas of difficulty. Treat each emotional pang as a thread that leads you into your inner landscape. You will find the spaces in you that need healing and care there. We will do boundary work in your inner world as well as in your outer world. You will reflect on how you learned to connect with others and will strengthen your internal boundaries, so you can set boundaries with other people more clearly and kindly.

Setting boundaries is difficult in part because it's hard to think that something we are going to say or do will hurt someone. It is also painful and angering to be disrespected or rejected when we try to say what is right for us. I'll say more about this in the pages to come, but for now, know that compassion soothes the brain. Self-compassion is essential. I, too, have struggled with setting boundaries that stick and have grappled with each type of boundary I describe in these pages. Take heart in these three facts: brains change, change takes time, and you are not alone.

It will be helpful to have a journal or a sketch pad by your side as you explore new ways of thinking about your mind, feelings, and relationships. Journaling and exploration exercises are included to help you learn to watch your own mind, become more curious and compassionate, and develop daily practices to transform how your brain perceives your level of protection. They are an opportunity for you to explore what your experiences have taught you about boundaries, build new ideas about how feelings work, and try out the practices to discover what will work for you. Throughout this book, I've included stories to illustrate the process for setting boundaries. (These stories are compilations of different moments from a variety of cases and interactions I have had with clients, interwoven for teaching purposes. They are not verbatim interactions, nor are they precise representations of any client I have seen.)

Take a breath, breathe out slowly, and offer this thought to yourself: *Setting boundaries with others can be complicated, hard work; it is also a set of skills that are doable.* Notice what happened inside when you offered yourself that thought. Throughout this book, I want you to be curious about how the mind creates the self over time.

I think of self like a river. If you come to the edge of the valley and look at the river every day, it will mostly look the same day by day. But if you left and came back after twenty years, the river would look very different: the banks would have shifted, the topography changed, the tree line transformed. If you walk down and put your hand in the water, you will feel how the river changes through time, moment to moment. The flow is in constant motion; you can feel it. Rains come and swell the river and shift it in new ways; drought comes and slims the river down. To watch the mind is like putting your hand in that river, experiencing how the flow of sensations, thoughts, and feelings changes you through time. And to read these pages is to perhaps change the way that river flows, as you let the information you learn change how you think, feel, and, ultimately, act. I feel grateful to be invited to be a part of your journey. I hope what these pages offer is helpful to you as you achieve greater empowerment and peace.

CHAPTER 1

Boundaries and Your Brain

The curious paradox is that when I accept myself just as I am, then I can change.

—Carl Rogers

There's an old saying that goes, "Clear is kind. Unclear is unkind." This saying is a good compass for boundary work. Many of us are taught to be nice, to not hurt others by sharing our truth. That is a formula for disconnection. When we risk being clear with others, we have feelings of both fear and empowerment, such as nervousness, worry, clarity, relief, joy, and authenticity. When we do not risk being clear with others, we have the feelings that go along with hiding our truth: self-doubt, resentment, longing, shame, anger, loneliness, and sadness. These feelings, if unresolved and unchecked, are likely to prompt behaviors full of contempt and defensiveness, or actions that are unloving. Boundaries help us to clearly communicate who we are, in alignment with our values. It may seem paradoxical, but boundaries help us to connect to others. Doing boundary work is an act of love for both self and other people.

This book is designed to teach you how to set boundaries so that you can live in that empowered space—feeling both safer in yourself and truly connected to other people. Throughout, you will learn about how the brain works on a neurobiological level, and how to relate to your own mind and feelings intentionally. You'll meet other people using the tools offered in this book and hear their stories and dialogues as we go along. You'll see them risking vulnerability and connection, trying and messing up, trying and succeeding. You'll gain the tools to empower yourself and respond to others with calm clarity from an integrated brain state.

Some Brain Basics

To keep it simple, let's think about the brain in two main states: integrated and unintegrated. An *integrated brain state* is a slower and more nuanced brain state in which networks from various areas of the brain share information. The brain perceives general okay-ness and therefore knows that there is enough time to be in this more complex way of functioning. In an integrated brain state, you can synthesize information from many different neural networks into a cohesive whole. When your brain is more integrated, you are more responsive than reactive and can have a nuanced view of things and access to creativity and resources for problem solving. When your brain senses that you and your body are physically and psychologically safe, it will take the time to connect and communicate with all of its parts, to integrate them.

When your brain is *unintegrated*, you are more reactive. You move into black-and-white thinking, lose access to nuance and creativity, and make choices hastily, without a lot of forethought. Unintegrated mental states are great for reacting with speed, because the vast neural networks do not take the time to share much information with each other, and the parts of your brain that move fastest hold sway. This helps your body move quickly, without deliberation or thought. That is ideal if your toddler is chasing a ball that's heading toward the street. You don't think about what to do, but just run and pick him up. *Thank you, reactive, unintegrated brain state. That speed was helpful.* Reacting with that same speed in a challenging conversation with someone you care about, however, may not have such good results. That conversation might be better served with the nuance and creativity of a responsive and integrated brain.

When you feel more protected and you trust yourself, your brain will let you be more resourced, more nuanced, more responsive. When you do not feel protected, your brain makes a fast decision not to pause. This reaction is helpful when faced with a true attacker. It is not helpful when having a conversation with someone you love, because your brain goes on autopilot; big, defensive reactions are common, and feeling regret later about what you did or said is normal.

We've all had moments when we were being reactive even though we knew that being less reactive would have been more helpful. Sometimes you can even watch yourself doing something that you know will make a situation worse, but you can't stop it from happening in the moment. This is being in an unintegrated brain state.

The brain responds to moments of perceived danger and hurt by becoming less integrated, and it responds to moments when you feel protected and okay by becoming more integrated. This is where boundary work comes in. Your boundaries give you added protection, which helps your brain guess that you have the time to slow down, synthesize information, and connect with all your knowledge and awareness. In an integrated state, you can draw on more of what you know.

We support an integrated brain state by practicing boundary setting. Both *internally*, within ourselves, and *externally*, with others, boundary setting builds the feeling of protection which our brains respond to with increased integration. Better boundaries are the secret to a responsive, fully accessible brain.

Throughout this book, you'll meet individuals and couples who are learning to set boundaries. Let's look at Steve and Nihal processing a moment in which they were both reactive.

Process with Steve and Nihal

Steve and Nihal had figured out how to move their marriage into a great place. "We laugh all the time now," Nihal smiled at me.

"Let's talk about the other night, though," Steve said. "She's right, we are doing so much better. But I get worried when we have a rumble, like maybe we will fall back into old patterns."

Steve described a moment when he asked Nihal if he could take the kids to his mother's house without her. "I did it so badly, though," he said. "I was mumbling and not being clear and not looking at her. I asked at the very last minute. Then she was mad at me, feeling rejected. Then I actually begged her to come after all, because I couldn't deal with how much I hurt her."

In Nihal's view, Steve had hinted that her presence made things harder for him. But he didn't come out and say it—she had to "drag the truth out of him." Then, when he changed his mind about her coming, it didn't feel like an invitation. She felt he couldn't handle her upset feelings.

"We did a great job of fixing it later," Steve said, "but I just wish we could get to a place where moments like that didn't happen at all." Steve turned to Nihal. "The truth is that sometimes I do want to go to my mom's without you. I am sorry I didn't just say that and you had to drag it out of me."

"It's not all you," Nihal said. "I get defensive with you and make it hard for you to say things outright. I make things hard for you with your mom, too. I end up fighting with her a lot."

Steve was nervous about sharing a request with Nihal, and in doing so sideways, he ended up in an interaction that felt painful. Nihal got defensive when Steve first shared his request with her, which made the interaction scary and hard for both of them. Steve had a fantasy hope of having a relationship where pain could be avoided, which made his communication unclear. Instead of that impossible stance, he could work on naming his requests and boundaries clearly—and feeling protected enough to have challenging conversations without getting reactive and losing his head. During their repair, they were able to be more responsive, which made things go better for both of them.

Let me clarify. I do not mean to say that a reactive, unintegrated brain is bad and that a responsive, integrated brain is good. It's not so simple. We need both. When you are in danger, it's better to move into a more reactive state; under threat, it is often better to act first and feel and think about it later. The problem is that our brains aren't always great at feeling protected and so might move into an unintegrated state when an integrated one might be more helpful.

Sometimes we feel hurt, worried, scared, or helpless, and act from an unintegrated brain state when it's possible that things are actually not so dangerous. They may be painful and hard, but they are fundamentally okay. Our lives and relationships might greatly improve if we were able to access our integrated mind in those situations. So how do we get there?

Improving your boundaries can help. When you walk around this world feeling relatively centered because you trust yourself to keep yourself both protected and connected with others in many situations, you will be in a responsive, integrated state more often (Siegel 2020).

We become reactive when we don't have sufficient internal protection—in other words, we don't have solid internal structures for how to think about our own needs and how to communicate them. This isn't something most of us are taught, but it is essential. Building those structures will protect us in interactions. When we establish clear internal ways of thinking about our needs and how to communicate them, both our interactions with others and our experiences during difficult moments will transform for the better.

Being able to watch your own mind will help you in shifting from reactivity to responsiveness. Your mind is processing information through sensations, movements, thoughts, feelings, and images all of the time. It helps to notice what is happening in your mind. If you are already a mindfulness meditator, you know what I am talking about. If you are saying to yourself, "Ugh, I hate meditation," don't worry. There isn't any meditation in this book. You can learn to watch your own mind in many ways, and the inner exploration exercises in each chapter will help you increase this skill.

Every mind is different. If you find that your mind communicates to you in thoughts better than feelings, you will learn to witness your thoughts. If you are a feelings processor, your emotions may come to your awareness first. If you are a sensation processor or find truth in movement or think in metaphors and images, go with what is natural to you. I invite you to build your witnessing practice by noticing all of the various ways your mind communicates with you—they are all worthy. So you might journal, or dance, or draw, or make collages as you answer these questions. In the invitations to explore, I will invite you to take out your journal, but if you want to draw or move instead—or in addition to writing—trust yourself and do what feels right to you.

An invitation to explore: Take out your journal and make some notes about your own experiences with reactivity (unintegrated brain states) and responsiveness (integrated brain states), using these prompts:

A time when I was really integrated and responsive was…

- *When I think of that time, I feel…*

- *Thoughts coming up for me are…*

- *What I notice in my body is…*

- *Memories, impressions, or images coming up for me are…*

A time when I was reactive but didn't want to be was…

- *When I think of that time, I feel…*

- *Thoughts coming up for me are…*

- *What I notice in my body is…*

- *Memories, impressions, or images coming up for me are…*

A time when I was reactive and that helped me was...

- *When I think of that time, I feel...*

- *Thoughts coming up for me are...*

- *What I notice in my body is...*

- *Memories, impressions, or images coming up for me are...*

A time when I set boundaries in a way that didn't work was...

- *When I think of that time, I feel...*

- *Thoughts coming up for me are...*

- *What I notice in my body is...*

- *Memories, impressions, or images coming up for me are...*

A time when I set boundaries that did work was...

- *When I think of that time, I feel...*

- *Thoughts coming up for me are...*

- *What I notice in my body is...*

- *Memories, impressions, or images coming up for me are...*

Good work bearing witness to your own mind!

Your Psychological Floor

If you build your boundaries and the ability to communicate them clearly, and get familiar with your own mind, emotions, and patterns, you will be able to respond from an integrated brain state even when situations are hard or conflictual. This requires watching your mind and getting to know your psychological floor.

The *psychological floor* is a concept we will draw on throughout this book. What is it? Well, we walk through the world being influenced by all the things we have ever learned without consciously knowing it. The things we have learned feel as real to us (and as outside of our conscious attention) as the floor we walk on. All of those things are processed in the subcortical brain—the densely wired part of the brain in the middle and base (Imms et al. 2021). This brain system moves faster than language to deliver information and feelings to us.

Think of it like this. If you saw a friend set her tea down half off the edge of the table, you would not have to slowly move through each of these thoughts: *On this planet, gravity is a thing, and that tea will fall and spill, because I am guessing Joan doesn't see what she just did, unless I alert us all to the issue and perhaps stop the spill.* Of course not. Instead, you would not hesitate to speak or to move to grab the cup. You might not even be aware of an emotion or thought while you were catching the cup, though emotions and thoughts are happening simultaneously with your reaction.

Knowledge of gravity is a kind of emotional knowing in your psychological floor. But it is not the only emotional knowing there; you also have an emotional knowing about what spilling something means. Perhaps you got laughed at and felt shame when you spilled. Maybe people around you reacted in fear or panic. Maybe you were punished when things went wrong. Perhaps you grew up in a house where spilling was no big deal, or maybe your family just thought it was funny.

What you know from the past is processed in your subcortical brain and will determine how you react to this situation. For example, you might call out in a panicky voice, "Joan, the cup!" Or you might ignore it and hope someone else will call attention to it if you have learned that calling attention to yourself leads to hurt. Maybe you roll your eyes and smile as you reach over to pick up the cup and put it further back on the table. The way you interact with the world is deeply influenced by your history.

How relationships feel, how people perceive you, your sense of who you are, what boundaries mean and whether or not boundaries are safe to assert in relationships with others are all relevant to this boundaries journey. In fact, all of your previous knowledge is organized in your subcortical brain into neural networks that are processing understandings about the world that have a felt sense of being true (Barrett 2017; Ecker, Ticic, and Hulley 2012.)

When I talk about your brain's neural networks, I'm referring to how millions of neurons fire together in patterns of activation over time. You may have heard the phrase "What fires together, wires together." This means that the more frequently you respond in a certain way, the more likely you will respond the same way in the future. So if you expect that speaking up gets you nowhere, and you have learned not to speak up, every time you repeat this pattern will make it more likely that you will not speak up in the future. Patterns can be hard to change, but they are changeable. So if you have some previous learnings about boundaries that aren't working for you, all the practices here are designed to help you do the work of changing your neural network firing patterns.

These patterns hold multidimensional information, a dynamic mix of emotion, sensation, thought, imagery, ancestral experiences, embodiment, and prediction all woven together. From this dense weave of different kinds of awareness, the neural networks give us something. In neurobiological research, we don't have a single word for this something, because our understanding of how the brain works is so new. I call it *emotional knowings*, because what we receive is not so much thought of as *known*, and it just feels true and real. In this interweaving of your knowings is your aliveness and your unique way of perceiving the world.

That brings us back to the psychological floor. Let's go a little more deeply into this metaphor now. Imagine that every moment of every day, you are walking across a floor made up of tiles of different emotional knowings and rugs on top of that floor that are full of emotional knowings as well (yep, it gets complex in there), and since you've been walking on the floor your whole life, for the most part, you ignore it. It is in this floor that you will find all that you know about taking things personally or not, how to set boundaries, and what would happen to you if you did. In this floor, you know how to stand up for yourself, if you can use your voice and your power, what power means, and what kindness feels like. There is nothing wrong with your psychological floor. It came to be because of real experiences you have had. Wanting to change it means you want to grow, not that something is wrong with you.

The neocortex—the very thin outside layer of the brain that's wrinkly and a few millimeters thick—receives information from both what is happening now and your psychological floor and weaves those threads of information together to help you understand the world (Kandel 2006; Siegel 2020). Your brain looks at the world through history-colored glasses. Because of this wiring, it is helpful to look at your history—not just with your family of origin but also with peers, friends, partners, work associates, and other significant relationships—and the larger society in which you've lived to be able to see your boundary knowings more clearly.

Once you do, you can decide if any of those tiles or rugs need to change. The great news is that you can do a psychological floor remodel if you need to. You can change out a rug or go all the way to foundation repair, whatever is right for you.

Risking Real Connection

Closeness with others is made through vulnerability. I like Brene Brown's (2017) definition of vulnerability: it is anything involving risk and emotional exposure, without a certain outcome. This means that being vulnerable requires courage. And our brains are able to guide us to courageous action when we feel protected enough not to move into reactivity. If your protection, internally, is not strong enough, you will likely avoid vulnerability or do confusing moves that you intend to be connecting but are actually defensive and increase distance—like demanding a partner listen to you better. If you want closeness, closeness requires vulnerability. Vulnerability requires an integrated and responsive brain state. Doing internal boundary work is going to be a key to your success.

Keep these brain basics in mind as we turn our attention to how all this plays out in setting boundaries.

Four Types of Boundary

We will explore four main types of boundary: external, psychological, containing, and physical. Most people are never taught about the inner boundary work that can allow them to successfully hold external boundaries. It's time to change that. External boundaries are between you and other people, but psychological and containing boundaries are inner boundaries that support your external boundaries. Physical boundaries can be both internal and external. Let's explore each one of these more.

External Boundaries

When most folks use the word "boundaries," they mean external boundaries. An *external boundary* is your ability to let others know what is and is not okay with you and to match your actions to that communication. A good external boundary will help you respond to others' behaviors with empowerment and integrity.

External boundaries are entirely about your communication and behavior in response to the behaviors of others. To establish these boundaries, you communicate with others about how they are affecting you and what you will do in response. Establishing good external boundaries does not require receiving permission or approval from others. Establishing an external boundary does not mean that you are demanding others act in a particular way. You are simply letting them know what *you* will do if something is happening that doesn't feel okay to you.

As a simple example, if a friend is texting you in harsh and unwelcome ways, you might state several things: that this kind of messaging does not feel okay to you; that you want to stay in contact with your friend because you care about them; and that if the harsh texting continues, you will take a break from connecting with them for the rest of the day.

Psychological Boundaries

A *psychological boundary* refers to a kind of an inner boundary that separates your mind from other people's minds inside your own head. Building awareness of your psychological boundary is a way to keep your mind protected from being influenced too much by the minds of others and also to open yourself to influence that is helpful. This boundary allows you to choose what to take in. You will learn how to use a visual mental image of a boundary in your daily life to remind you of your personal agency and protection. An active psychological boundary also helps to keep other people safe when interacting with you, because it will help you listen to them with acceptance and without trying to change or control them. When you use your psychological boundary, others will be unlikely to know you are doing so.

Here's a brief example. Your partner has a different feeling than you do about an interaction with some friends and is critical of how you behaved. You imagine your boundary image between the two of you to help your brain stay integrated and not become overwhelmed by the differences in your perspectives. This helps challenging conversations go more smoothly, because you can listen less defensively while staying true to yourself and remaining clear about your own perspective.

Containing Boundaries

The *containing boundary* is an inner boundary that can be especially helpful when reacting in the moment may not reflect your best, most value-driven self. Activating your containing boundary involves adding a mental and time pause between what you feel and what you do. During that pause, you remember a key word that reminds you of your values and make a physical gesture to offer yourself compassion. Using this boundary allows you to pause, feel, think, and consciously choose a response. When you have a containing boundary that works for you, your communication and behaviors will match your intentions in how you relate to others. The containing boundary is a way of staying aligned with your personal integrity and how you want to behave in relationships.

You bolster your containing boundary when you practice becoming more aware of yourself and what you really feel and think, and shifting the ways you behave in light of this awareness. This practice activates the pathways between your prefrontal cortex (a part of your neocortex just behind your forehead) and your subcortical mind (Siegel 2020). Strengthening this boundary will also shift the behavior others witness in you. And when your behaviors align with your hopes and your integrity more frequently, you will trust yourself more.

For example, when a coworker cuts you off in a meeting for the third time, you might pause, breathe, do your compassion gesture privately, silently remind yourself of your values, and then decide how you want to reply. This will help you speak up for yourself but not say things you may later regret.

Physical Boundaries

Finally, the *physical boundary* is your ability to experience your physical body as safe when you are relatively safe, to protect your physical well-being, and to create more safety when needed and such action is possible. Your physical boundary relates to what feels good to you and what doesn't in terms of physical contact and closeness with others, so it is both internal and external. Awareness of this boundary increases your experience of physical protection by guiding you to become more cognizant of your relative safety in the moment. It also prompts you to increase your external boundaries to align with what your body needs to feel safe in various situations. When that happens, your feeling of protection deepens (Levine 2015).

Your physical boundary helps you decide how close or far you want to be from others and what kind of touch you want or don't want. This is especially helpful for those who have a history of having their boundaries violated by others or being unaware of what feels good to them or not. Physical boundary repair is generally done away from difficult situations, where our brains are often on guard and need to be unintegrated to increase our safety. When you are in a safer space, you might mentally outline your whole body with a certain color to restore a sense of physical well-being. With an awareness of the safety of your body, it is easier to be clear with others about what does and doesn't feel good.

Your psychological, containing, and physical boundaries interweave to create an internal landscape that supports you when you set external boundaries with others, so that they stick. As you do this work, using these boundaries will help you make changes in three areas: how your mind works, how you talk to yourself, and how you communicate with others. These practices will also change your psychological floor.

Every one of the tools in this book is a practice. It is one thing to understand the practices intellectually but putting them into action takes intention and repetition. As you embark on these practices, it's important that you keep in mind the pacing of true and deep brain change, which is what we are after. It takes only three to four weeks to develop a practice, but it will take longer than that to automatically regulate your feelings, and it will take two years or more for these practices to transform your brain in a permanent way so that it feels natural and second nature to function with all of your boundaries intact (Siegel 2010b).

To keep your work going, two things will be needed: patience and celebration. Be patient with your brain and celebrate every time you learn something new or employ a new practice, even when you think you didn't do it right. Once you understand how boundaries work and how you can actively employ them, this work will deepen throughout your lifespan.

Now let's talk about healthy boundaries.

What Is a Healthy Boundary?

You can think of boundaries as being on a spectrum: one end is rigid, and the other end is porous.

boundaries

rigid   porous

On the rigid side, very little information—in the form of feelings, thoughts, and ideas from other people—comes in. Likewise, very little of your feelings, thoughts, and ideas go out toward others. On the porous side, a whole lot of information goes out—you share your feelings, thoughts, and ideas liberally—and a whole lot comes in. You easily take in other people's feelings, thoughts, and ideas as true.

There is no particular spot on the spectrum, or a particular behavior or rule, that defines healthy boundaries. Rather, I like to define healthy boundaries in terms of internal flexibility and responsiveness. There are times when you'll know that a more rigid boundary is best and times when you'll know a more porous boundary is best.

For example, you may be in a toxic work environment that you can't leave, and you wall yourself off against your boss's insults. That rigid wall protects you against taking anything they say to heart. You stop listening, and your boundary, impenetrable, protects you.

Here's another example. During a romantic evening with a partner, when you are sharing deep feelings, or when experiencing music, art, literature, or talking with a close group of friends, having a more porous boundary will allow you to be moved by them. It will help you open yourself up to experience and being more influenced by others.

Healthy boundaries are not about figuring out how to stay right in the middle of the rigid–porous spectrum. Healthiness is about knowing what home base feels good to you; maybe that's in the middle, or maybe it's more toward one side or the other of the rigid–porous spectrum. Then, it's trusting that you can move away from that home base in response to the moment, your environment, and your current needs.

Finding Home Base

You likely have a home base somewhere in between the polarities on each boundary spectrum: external, psychological, containing, and physical. In later chapters, we will explore your personal spectrums more fully. It is up to you to determine what feels right for you. If you are introverted, you might lean a bit more rigid on the containing boundary spectrum; if you are an empath, you might lean more toward the porous end psychologically. There is no right or wrong way—there is only your way, for now—and an awareness that your way may change as a result of learning and through the years.

That said, you may also sense that your current home base on any of these boundary spectrums will need to change for your life to feel more empowered and safer. In the end, once you know your current home-base spot on each boundary spectrum and feel secure knowing why and how you tend to land at that spot, you can begin developing skills to move that position if that is what is right for you. Being able to move positions on the spectrum in response to changing needs within you and to the environment around you is very helpful.

When you think about boundaries, imagine that yours become more porous when it feels right to you and more rigid when you need them to be. Know that different situations require different internal boundary protection. Your flexibility and your responsiveness will make your boundaries healthy. Defining for yourself what feels right for you, both within yourself and in your relationships with others, will help you gain the trust and empowerment you need to set boundaries that stick. Over time, you will find the home base that aligns with who are and who you aim to be.

Boundaries, Relativity, and Identity

It's crucial to recognize that boundaries are going to signify different things to each of us based on our identities. Our positions and locations socially, as well as our cultural identities, skin colors, sexual orientations, physical abilities, genders, and many other factors, all play a role in how rigid or porous our boundaries are at any given time—and how we interpret the boundaries of others. For example, different cultures have their own norms around physical boundaries and physical touch. The same is true of emotional expression and contact. A fairly middle-ground sense of a containing boundary in one culture might seem extremely rigid, buttoned-up, or inexpressive in the context of another. As you move from one country to another, one space to another, or one group of people to another, you may sense yourself naturally shifting in response to the cultural expectations and values of the place you are in.

It's also true that asserting boundaries is safer for some people than for others due to differing levels of privilege. I will always urge you to trust your gut. For example, if you have a lived experience of being frequently marginalized or criminalized by our society, then you may have real safety choices to make about when to speak up and when to lean into rigidity as protective. If you are a person of color amongst many white people in a white supremacist culture, then having a more rigid psychological boundary can be wise, because many things said to you and about you will not be true. Boundaries can be an act of resistance. If I, a white cisgender woman, am listening to a person more marginalized than myself, I want to make my boundaries more porous, so I can take in more of their experience and believe them when they are sharing their truth with me.

I do not have answers about which spot along the spectrum will serve you best in different contexts. I trust that within you there is wisdom about moving along the boundary spectrums in ways that will serve you. In these pages, you will find tools that will help you find that wisdom so that you can live with as much protection and integrity as is possible in the landscapes of inequality that exist on our planet. Use your boundaries to respect and protect your true and unique humanity.

When you are assessing where you are on any of the boundary spectrums, think about what you have learned in your history, or even what generations of your family may have learned and that may have been passed to you through ancestry. It is most likely that whatever you learned was adaptive and wise at some point in your life—that is, it brilliantly helped you adapt to the conditions you were in. There is nothing wrong with where you have been or where you are.

Mostly, folks end up where they are on the various boundary spectrums because it somehow helped them get through life. The question is not, *Does this mean something is wrong with me?* The question to ask is, *Is this way I have learned working for me now?* If it is not working, be grateful for that way of getting to where you are now, and use the tools in this book to create a new way.

The next chapter will take you through six steps to setting an external boundary. It is the core process you will use when you need to set a boundary with someone else, so you can make your life more safe, empowered, and peaceful.

CHAPTER 2

Six Steps to Setting an External Boundary

Boundaries have nothing to do with whether you love someone
or not… Boundaries teach people how to treat you and they teach
you how to respect yourself.

—Cheryl Strayed

There are going to be many times in your life when you will need to make
an external boundary with someone: informing them of what is okay and
not okay with you and letting them know what you will do in response to
things that are not okay. This chapter will teach you a six-step process for
setting an external boundary. Some of these steps may be more challenging
for you than others. Take note in your mind or in your journal when you
come upon parts that are particularly challenging, because those hard spots
will guide you to places where you can change in big ways, and places where
your internal work needs the most support and attention, as you learn to set
boundaries that stick.

Before starting on the six steps, it's important to understand the difference between requests, complaints, demands, and boundaries. They can be tricky to tell apart.

Requests Vs. Demands and Complaints

People often confuse the meaning of setting boundaries with making requests, demands, or complaints. Each of the latter focuses on what someone else does whereas setting a boundary is about what you do. As an example, prior to setting a boundary, it can be a good move to make a clear request. Making a request is when you ask for someone to collaborate with you and change something to help you get a need or want met. You make a request when you want someone to do something different or new. Sometimes the change you are asking for is a big deal, and other times it might be minor. You are worthy of making requests and hoping for others to meet many of them. Making a request is not selfish or mean. Sometimes people will shift, and sometimes they won't. If you are asking for a behavior change in the other person, it is a direct request.

Afterward, if the person does not change their behavior, and it is still not okay to you—if something is truly unacceptable—I recommend setting an external boundary rather than making a demand for behavior change, which can be controlling. A boundary does not try to force behavior change in others, but it lets them know what you will do if something unacceptable is happening. Sometimes this does prompt behavior change in others, which can be a welcome relief.

Another confusion I often hear is between requests and complaints. A complaint can sound like, "This thing you do is bad because…" A complaint is a way of making it clear that you don't like something without risking the vulnerability of requesting what you want to happen instead. If you find yourself complaining, use your containing boundary to pause and wonder what your request might be. Try sharing that instead of complaining, and see what happens.

In partnership, work relationships, parenting, and friendships, we are often hopeful for easy cooperation. Sometimes this occurs. Sometimes it doesn't. Sometimes we make demands instead of requests. If you make a demand, you are insisting on yes for an answer. The problem with this is you're assuming you can control another person, but the truth is you can't. Suffering often comes when we put our will up against reality.

Generally, if behavior change is what you are hoping for (and inside of most boundaries there is a hope for behavior change), you can try making requests before you decide on a boundary action. Requests are relational and give the person the opportunity to change their behavior. You can also do your inner boundary work with your physical, psychological, and containing boundaries to help you discern what behavior or situation is not okay with you and what needs to be addressed.

When to Set a Boundary

If, after making a request and doing your inner work, you are still clear that you need to set a boundary to take care of yourself, then you can let the other person know what is and is not okay with you and what you will do to take care of yourself. This is both an opportunity for behavior change and a message about how you plan to take care of yourself. It lets the other person know the relational consequences of not changing their behavior. It gives them the autonomy to make their decisions with full awareness of what will happen if they choose to continue without a change.

You can set a boundary while being kind and respectful toward yourself and kind and respectful toward other people. Being kind is not the same as being nice, caretaking, or even being calm. By *kind*, I mean being thoughtful about how you affect others and being aware of this as you choose your words and actions. Sometimes you will want to be gentle and soft; with other people you will want to be quite stern while also staying respectful of their humanity. Boundaries between yourself and others will guide you to respond to them in ways that are clear and compassionate.

What would happen if you navigated your relational life with requests and boundaries rather than demands? Instead of "getting" other people to do what you want them to do, you would ask them to shift. You can be incredibly clear with yourself about what your deal breakers are, so that you can say what is not okay and therefore set boundaries instead of making demands in ways that try to control others.

Boundaries Are About What You Do

When you execute a boundary with someone, you are letting them know what you will do, not what you want them to do. This is empowering! To keep your boundaries, you aren't relying on anyone else to act a certain way or respect your limits. It is something you and you alone are in charge of.

This can also be hard to hear. The reality is that you cannot control any other person. You can influence a situation through your actions and words, yes. Of course, there will be moments when you successfully execute a boundary and change happens in response—change that really works for you. On the other hand, when you set a great external boundary, the outcome may bring sadness or pain. You may have to step away from a connection or end an encounter or relationship. Even in those moments, I see this work bring people pride and reassurance, because they are behaving in ways that are aligned with their integrity and worth.

Here's an example of how boundaries are about what you do, not about getting others to behave in certain ways. Liam is putting his kids to bed and says, "It is quiet time now, boys. If you can stop talking, I will stay and sing you a song. If you do not stop talking, then Daddy will leave the room for five minutes."

Notice here that Liam is saying what he will do in response to what is okay with him and what he will do in response to what is not okay with him. If his sons keep talking, then Liam will leave the room, as he said. Liam also knows his sons love when their dad sings to them, so it's likely they'll choose to stop talking when he makes this boundary.

Here's another scenario. Delphine's partner is often loud when they disagree. In a moment when things are calm, she says, "Sometimes when we are disagreeing your voice gets loud in a way that doesn't feel okay for me. When that happens, I am going to hold up my hand and ask for you to use a softer voice. If it's still not okay for me after that, I am going to take a twenty-minute time-out and we can try to finish our talk later."

If, in their next disagreement, Delphine's partner raises her voice, then Delphine will hold up her hand to pause and ask her partner to be softer. If her partner does use a quieter tone of voice (even while rolling her eyes), it will show that she was able to take in and accept Delphine's request. If her partner continues to raise her voice, then it will be time for Delphine to execute her boundary and take a twenty-minute time-out. This is an external boundary because Delphine is responding to what is not okay with her with her actions as well as her words. Delphine's actions are in alignment with what is and is not okay with her. The more we shift, the more likely it is that our partners will shift, though there is no guarantee that they will. If you want big shifts to happen in your relationships, it will be helpful to use your inner and external boundary work to support you in having the difficult conversations and giving the time necessary to support big changes.

Folks often ask, "How will I know if I should set this boundary, or how do I know if it is healthy?" The only person who can really answer that is you. As a guide, you can ask yourself this question: *Is something going on that is not okay with me?* If the answer to that question is yes, then it might be important to come up with a clear and kind way to respond. Being clear and kind is a complex task, of course. Deciding what's kind and clear in a given situation means figuring out how to respect your own needs and desires while also respecting others' needs and intrinsic value. This complex task is what we'll work through in this chapter. The key to keep in mind now is that an external boundary is when you can say to yourself: *I respond to what is not okay with me with clarity in my words and actions.*

Before reading further, think about something that is not working for you. It could be that someone in your life is behaving in ways that do not feel okay, or it could be something that's causing resentment and, no matter what you have tried, you haven't been able to make it change.

An invitation to explore: Answer these questions to explore something that is not okay for you.

- What is the situation or main issue?

- What is not going well? Is there something that you are holding resentment about? Is someone doing something that is not okay?

- When you think about this issue, what feelings, sensation, images, and thoughts do you notice?

Focus on this situation as you explore how to set up an external boundary.

Six Steps to Setting an External Boundary

This section gives you the opportunity to explore six steps to setting an external boundary, in your mind and journal, before you move this into action in your life with other people. As you work through the six steps, notice which parts feel hard for you. This will help you home in on how to use this method in the ways that are most transformative in your own personal life.

Step 1: Find Your Big Why

Finding your big why means identifying the deepest reasons why you need and want a boundary, and what will change for the better when it is established. The *big why* is a good reason to do hard things.

Doing something new is hard. Your brain likes habit and not rocking the boat. To follow through with doing this new (hard) thing, you need enough emotional power, enough "oomph," to make it worth all this work.

Let's listen as Tammy finds hers. This scenario takes place in my therapy office.

Process with Tammy

Tammy wanted to make a shift with her friend Steph. Steph was often late to engagements and would also frequently cancel at the last minute. Tammy felt anger and hurt when this happened, and she thought such treatment was disrespectful.

"When I was growing up, if I was late my parents told me I was being disrespectful, so I'm really careful not to be late," Tammy said. "I just don't like it. It hurts my feelings. I get pissed. But I roll over and just take it."

"So far, you haven't said anything to your friend?" I asked.

"I haven't. I mean, I might roll my eyes or complain that she's late, but nothing changes and then I avoid her calls. I am so mad, I end up being passive-aggressive. But she won't change, no matter what I do." Tammy sighed. "She does this with everyone. She's even been fired for it."

"You might be right about that. She might not change, but you can. Think about the last time she was late," I suggested.

"Okay, this week, I sat at the restaurant for twenty minutes by myself." Tammy clenched her jaw.

"And what do you feel right now as you think about that?"

"I am pissed."

"Sure, and anything else?"

"In the moment, I was afraid I messed up—that I got the time wrong. I was also hurt, like she must not care about me."

"Good work. So when this friend is late, you feel angry and hurt and scared, like panic. So, this behavior of hers is affecting you in ways that are not okay?"

"Is it okay that it's not all right with me?" Tammy asked.

"You get to decide what isn't okay with you," I answered. "What is it like to see that you treat yourself badly in this situation: you act like something is okay when it isn't, and when you don't say anything, you feel resentful and avoid her? Am I understanding what it's like?"

"Yeah. It's bad," Tammy answered. "I guess I am treating both of us badly. She's messing up, but then I am messing up right back."

"And if you don't change anything, what is the hope?" I asked.

"The hope is that I don't have to have a hard conversation. I hate confrontation. But doing nothing about it is not worth it. I think about this a lot. I give it a ton of energy," Tammy answered.

"So if you put into words why this isn't okay with you, what would those words be?" I asked her.

"I don't want to be treated like I don't matter. Even if that isn't what she means by it, it's how it feels to me, and I hate it."

"Great! Now let's find your *big why*."

"What do you mean?" Tammy asked.

"In our world, we often focus on what's not working, but not so much on what we really want for ourselves. I find that when our big why is positive, it really aligns with who we want to be, and it gives us a good reason to do hard things. So what is a good reason for doing this hard thing? What do you want to get out of it that is a positive for you?"

"I get it," Tammy said. "I want my friends to know the real me, and I want to take care of myself."

Tammy did a great job of finding a big why that would work for her. Now let's find yours. Remember, you are about to make a shift, and shifts are hard, so it's time to find a really good reason to do something hard. Bring into your mind the difficulty you are focusing on. Then get out your journal.

An invitation to explore: Answer these questions for yourself as you explore your big why.

- When you think of the situation that is not okay, what feelings and thoughts come up?

- What is happening is causing some sort of pain, discomfort, or fear. When you let this become clear, what do you notice?

- What are the costs of continuing to do things this way?

- What are the benefits of continuing to do things this way?

Now try turning your big why into a statement:

- What are the words for your big why? Try to keep it short and simple.

- Shift your words to a more positive perspective if you need to. What good are you going to get out of this boundary?

- Read your statement aloud. How does it feel in your body and mind when you own your big why?

Finding the big why is often the longest of the six steps. Keep working at finding yours until you have the words down that feel emotionally potent enough to support you. Once you have your big why, you can move on to step two.

Step 2: Define Your Action

When you are setting a boundary with someone, it can be helpful to find, choose, and practice what you are going to say ahead of time. Your words will let the other person know what is and is not okay with you and share the actions that you will take if the *not okay* thing happens. This can be kind and relational rather than harsh: think caring and firm at the same time, taking "caring" to mean that you're thinking of yourself and the other person respectfully; you're not setting a boundary to be punitive toward the other person. You can think about it as a way to share your truth with deep respect for both yourself and the other person at the same time.

In order to find your boundary words, you will have to clarify for your-self the action you will take in the future if or when the thing that is not okay occurs. In this step, you clarify and define for yourself what actions you will take and decide upon a short, loving, clear, firm way to share your intention with the other person. Let's follow Tammy's story a little further to see how it might work.

"Now that you know your *why*, let's move onto what you are going to do about it," I said to Tammy.

"I want Steph to show up on time," Tammy responded.

"I understand. But asking her to show up is a request, not a boundary. You've already made that request in the past. A boundary is about what you are going to do. How important is this friendship to you? Do you want to keep it?" I asked.

"Yes," Tammy said.

"Okay, so what would you be willing to do to protect yourself? To keep yourself well, even though her lateness probably won't change?" I asked.

"I could leave if she's more than ten minutes late?" Tammy said in a tentative tone.

"Sure, you could choose not to wait longer than feels okay with you," I said. "You could only meet her in public spaces when there is a group getting together, so that you don't feel you are waiting on her, because you are enjoying hanging out with everyone."

"I could only meet her alone at my place, when it's a free afternoon, so I can just be living my life instead of waiting for her," Tammy said.

"Yes, it's the waiting on her that causes the stress for you, so you can set up ways to not wait, regardless of her being on time or not," I said. "How could you deliver this message with love and clarity and firmness? The message will probably have in it something about what is okay with you, something about what is not okay with you, and then an action."

"I don't even want to wait ten minutes, because there's too much history of this bothering me. So I think I just want to meet her out with groups and then at one of our places when we are one-on-one." Tammy paused. "Actually, I've met her at her place, and she's been late getting there too, so I just want to meet one-on-one at my place. Oh, my God, she is going to be so upset."

"We'll be working with responding to her feelings in steps three through six, so hang on. For now, you are just looking for words to share your clarity," I told her. "You want to meet her one-on-one only at your place or out in groups. What words feel right to you?"

"I could tell her, 'I love our friendship and I want to hang out. When you are late, it is hard for me, so from now on, when we hang out one-on-one, I only want to do that at my place where I have other things I can do until you get there.'"

Tammy found her way of sharing her boundary in her own words. Notice that it was short, only two sentences, and that Tammy did not try to manage her friend's feelings in her delivery of the boundary.

Are you ready to define your action? Use this journal exercise to find the right words for you.

An invitation to explore: Focus on the thing that is not okay, and use these questions to help form a statement that will communicate your boundary. Try to keep it short, so your final statement will be a sentence or two.

- What is okay with you in the situation?

- What is not okay with you in the situation?

- What actions are you willing to take in response to what is not okay with you?

- Think about how you want to show up in this relationship. How important is clarity to you? How important is kindness to you?

- Write down what you will say in one to two sentences.

- As you read what you wrote, notice how it feels in your body. What do you discover?

When you were defining your action, were you worried about how the other person would feel? If you were very worried, then you might have been told when you were young that boundaries are harmful or that you should put the feelings of others ahead of your own. If you got these messages, the psychological boundary work in chapter 3 will be helpful.

Maybe you found yourself wanting to share a ton, and that writing just two sentences was really hard, or maybe you are surprised by the idea that some people even worry about their words hurting someone else's feelings. If either of those are issues for you, then the containing boundary work in chapter 4 is going to be helpful. If, as you imagine saying the words, your body feels shaky or numb, the physical boundary work in chapter 5 will help. No matter what reaction you had, note it down for now, and then, when you feel ready, continue through the six steps.

Step 3: Anticipate Potential Responses

Step 3 is to anticipate potential responses: in other words, to make some guesses about how the other person might respond. What you anticipate is just a guess, and it is important that you hold it as only a hypothesis, so that you can be open to surprise when you actually share your boundary in real life.

Anticipating how another person will respond to your boundary is helpful because the emotions and behaviors of others may cue your brain to perceive that you are not okay. For example, you might flex or let go of your boundary when you don't want to or state your boundary in a harsher way than you wanted to. You might also experience their response as the other person not respecting your boundary. It is normal to experience feeling a little less safe in moments like this, and it's possible that your brain will become less integrated. By anticipating responses, we are working to support your brain being as integrated as possible during the experience of boundary setting.

It's not unusual for others to become unintegrated when you communicate a boundary; they might have difficult feelings and become reactive. They might worry about getting what they want or about how they have affected you, or about what you think of them. Often, the person on the other end will feel a shame flood, go into black-and-white binary thinking, become frustrated, or move into pleading or negotiation. When you anticipate their response and can prepare for it, it will be easier for you to support your brain integration and maintain your boundary.

> When Tammy started exploring her friend's possible response, she guessed, "Well, she might get mad and defensive. But she probably will try to tell me that she'll fix it, or that I should relax—but she'll say it in a panicky way."
>
> "Are you thinking you will tell her this in person or on the phone or in a text?" I asked.
>
> "I'd prefer to send it in a text, so I don't have to see her reaction," Tammy said. "But I think the next time we get together, I'll invite her to my house and tell her in person. It feels braver."
>
> "Okay," I said. "If she gets defensive, how will that sound?"
>
> "She would say, 'You need to relax. You can be so uptight.'"
>
> "And if she gets into fix-it mode, how would that sound?"
>
> "She'll say, 'I get it, I know, I will get better, I promise.'"

We continued our discussion, and in the end, Tammy came up with six different ways that Steph might respond to her two-sentence boundary statement.

Now you try—make some guesses about how the other person in your life might respond to your boundary statement.

An invitation to explore: Focus on the other person in your mind, and imagine stating your boundary out loud. Then make some guesses about what might happen.

- What might they be thinking when you say this?

- What might they be feeling when you say this?

- What are at least three different behaviors you might see in response to sharing your boundary?

- What might they say in response to your boundary?

Now that you have guessed what might happen, it is time to move on to taking care of yourself.

Step 4: Anticipate Your Own Reactions

The next step is to make some guesses about how *you* are going to react internally. If your reactions are likely to be big and difficult to soothe, you will want to do the work in chapters 3 through 5 before trying this in your life. For now, watch your mind so that you can notice how you will react when someone does not like your boundary, falls into a shame spiral, or shuts down in response to you communicating a boundary.

Tammy wrote down her list of the potential responses from her friend, then looked at them one at a time, and slowly noticed what came up for her. It is normal to have a completely different reaction inside to all the different potential responses. It is also normal for some of us to have the same response to all feedback we get when setting a boundary. Listen to Tammy's process so that you can start imagining how this will work for you.

"If she does the 'I'll fix it' thing, I think I would roll my eyes— yeah, she's never fixed this anywhere. It's like, why is she so blind to herself? I turn judgmental."

"Is that feeling in your body or more in your thoughts?" I asked.

"It's in my arms, like I want to shake her." Tammy tracked her body. "I am mad."

"Okay, so if she does this fix-it thing, you'll get mad, you will want to shake her, and you'll be judgmental. You also said that your friend might cry a lot and be inconsolable. Can you imagine her doing that? What would happen inside you then? What would you do in response?"

"Oh, I probably would tell her to never mind, that it's not a big deal." Tammy's eyes widened. "I tend to let go of my own needs when others are upset. My mom used to do that all the time."

Tammy did a great job of guessing what she would feel and even tracked a habit back to how it was growing up. Now, it's your turn. Take out your journal and work through how you would likely respond to the other person's various reactions to your boundary.

An invitation to explore: Look at your list of how the other person might behave in response to your boundary statement. Go slowly to focus on one possibility at a time. Then answer these questions for each possibility.

- What would your thoughts be like?

- What would happen in your body?

- What would you likely feel?

- What might you do in response?

Steps 3 and 4 add awareness of how the other person may respond to your boundary and how you might react in turn. Putting a pause between your internal experience and what you do next is essential if you want to maintain your boundary. This will take intentional self-soothing, with compassion toward yourself, which is the focus of the next step.

Step 5: Create a Self-Soothing Plan

In this step, you create a self-soothing plan that will support your brain staying integrated. This is important because the psychological floor you are walking on is likely to have some rugs of learned behavior and some knowings about what to do automatically when pushback happens, like when people around you are upset, angry, or shut down. If you create a self-soothing plan, you can stop that go-to behavior that might have kept you from sticking to your boundaries before. Knowing what you're likely to do and deciding what you'll do differently is a fantastic way to change the pattern. Ideally, this plan is short and easy to execute in a tense moment: a soothing phrase and compassionate gesture toward yourself. Tammy worked hers out like this.

"So if the anger and judgment comes, how are you going to greet it?" I asked.

"Well, usually, I'd let it shut me down," she answered.

"I agree," I told her. "And the key thing is, you are setting this boundary to stay closer with your friend and be kind to you at the same time. So, you have to decide, do you want to maintain this boundary with judgment? Does that energy help you?"

"I think it makes it all on her, instead of owning my part. I'm the one who never says anything and judges her silently, like she's such a mess," Tammy reflected. "Now I am judging myself. I feel like a big a-hole."

"Well, I'm guessing you got taught to judge others somewhere along the way. What would happen if you said to that judgment voice, 'You are right, it hurts when she does this. It's also not my life: she can live her life her way, and I can take care of me with this boundary.'"

"You want me to talk to myself?" Tammy asked.

"Yes, I do. If you greet your psychological floor with kindness and a plan, a lot can shift. You don't have to do it out loud. Just silently have a talk between yourself and you."

"Okay." Tammy closed her eyes briefly and then after a few moments her hand went to her heart.

"That's a compassionate gesture," I said. "Your hand on your heart."

"Yeah, I thought the words 'I've got this,' and then everything calmed down."

Tammy's self-soothing plan became a hand on her heart and thinking the words "I've got this" to herself. It turned out that having one plan worked for all of Tammy's different responses. It might be that you need more than one plan depending on what is stirred in you. Take a first pass at making your self-soothing plan now.

An invitation to explore: Focus on your list of how you will react inside, and find your self-soothing plan. It will be helpful if your plan is short and easy to do. Use these prompts:

- What usually soothes you when you are upset or unintegrated?

- What will you do to soothe yourself?

- How will you show compassion and care to yourself before, during, and after the boundary conversation?

- If your soothing plan had a gesture or movement, it might be…

- If your soothing plan had words, they might be…

Try to imagine all the reactions of the other person. Do you need additional soothing plans for the various reactions? If so, come up with as many plans as you need.

With your big why in mind, how important is it to you to commit to your self-soothing plan and your boundary?

Step 6: Say It Again and Follow Through

It is common for there to be a difficult emotional experience or push-back from the other person with whom you are setting a boundary. They might also continue to do the thing that is not okay with you. This will be when you will need to restate your boundary and follow through. It can help to practice this in your mind or out loud. If your boundary is challenged, there's no need to apologize or explain; just restate it and follow through.

Witness Tammy's practice so that you can get an idea of how this works.

Tammy imagined being in her living room and doing steps 1 through 5. When she got to step 3 (anticipating potential responses), she imagined a scenario in which her friend broke down in tears. Tammy's hand was on her heart. "Okay, now what?" she asked.

"Now, in the face of this, you are going to reassert the boundary briefly," I said.

"Okay." She took a deep breath. "I shouldn't soothe her?"

"You can if that feels good to you, and it could also come with a message of 'This isn't going to change my mind.'"

"Okay." Tammy thought for a minute. "I would sit next to her and give her a hug if she wanted. I've got it. I can say, 'Steph, this is who you are—being on time or shifting plans isn't a big deal to you. I love you as you are.'"

"Good work. And if she says, 'I promise I'll be more on time, and it'll be better?'" I asked.

"I would say 'That would be great, but I'm not going to change my mind on this. I love me too, and this is me taking care of myself.'"

"Then what would happen?" I asked.

"Well, nothing then. Then we'd likely laugh and hug it out, and move on. But maybe a week later, she would ask me to meet her at a restaurant in a text. I can imagine it being on a workday, when my time is tighter than hers because I work nine-to-five, and she doesn't," Tammy said.

"Okay, remember your big why, hand on heart, 'I got this.' Now, what do you text back?" I asked.

"I would text her, 'Still taking care of myself and respecting you being you. Let's meet over the weekend instead. I am home all day on Saturday, and you can come over anytime in the afternoon.' And I would send some sort of smiley tongue-out emoji." Tammy smiled. "That feels good. I feel like I am taking care of myself." She paused, and worry passed over her face. "Does it seem mean?"

"Does it seem mean to you?" I asked her.

"No. She might not like it, she might feel bad, but it's not mean. I am not being mean. I am taking care of me."

Now try this for yourself.

An invitation to explore: Focus on doing your soothing plan. Imagine how you are going to respond to the other person's strong emotions or to a pushback. Imagine how you will restate and follow through on your boundary.

- How do you feel? Do you want to offer compassion to the other person when they push back or react?

- What do you need to state, briefly, to reassert your boundary?

- Imagine restating your boundary. How do you feel?

- Imagine doing the action you said you would do in the face of things not being okay. How do you feel?

- If the boundary pushback comes days or weeks later, what will you do?

- How will you feel about yourself if you hold and follow through on your boundary? Notice anything that feels good and make a note of it.

Enacting the six steps will not always get you what you want. There's no guarantee you will get the outcome you want in a situation where you draw boundaries, because we can only control our own actions. However, you can intervene to set boundaries around what is and is not okay and protect yourself when things are not okay. This will be a gift to both you and others, because when you take care of you, you are treating yourself like you matter and will have more energy to be connected, generous, and present. When you take care of you, you have more to give.

If questions come up about how to handle boundaries when you are making a change, dealing with someone who repeatedly does not honor boundaries, or being faced with a rupture so big that it might end the relationship, note that those situations will be the focus of later chapters. For now, you have a map of how to do the work to make setting and executing boundaries with others more simple and clear.

Before moving on, it will be helpful to look at where you frequently land on your external boundary spectrum.

Your External Boundary Spectrum

When thinking about your external boundaries on a spectrum, let your mind explore a wide variety of scenarios from your past and present life. Do you lean more porous, or more rigid, or bounce from one end to the other? In what situations do you end up more rigid, and in what situations do you go more porous?

Here are some clues. If you spend more time on the far porous end of the boundary spectrum, you are likely not to set limits even when you want to. You might have a hard time knowing what is and isn't okay with you. You might set limits with others but then collapse them when pushed—or even when you're not being pushed, because you just feel obligated to do so. You might even be harsh with yourself in your own mind for being *weak* or letting others *walk all over you*.

If you spend more time on the far rigid end of the boundary spectrum, you may be likely to cut yourself off or wall off from others in response to behavior that does not feel okay. You might have low flexibility when it comes to what is acceptable in others and your tone may be harsh. You might set a boundary in your own mind without letting the other person know that it happened. That is, you might not tell them that you are reacting to something they did, and instead just put up a barrier to connection, without communicating what you actually want or giving the other person a chance to change.

There are times when rigidity can be adaptive, healthy, and necessary—for example, folks who have been hurt frequently may have learned to wall off if they get a sense that something similar is about to happen. You may wisely execute a boundary that stops interactions or walls you off from people who are psychologically or physically dangerous to you if they have given no evidence that they will change.

There are also times when flexing a boundary is a great idea. Maybe new information has come to your attention that changes how you experience a situation, or perhaps something shifted internally and you genuinely changed your mind. Being flexible and being porous are not the same thing: being *flexible* is deciding to shift your assessment of what is okay with you and not okay with you.

It is common to feel resentment toward others if you are on either extreme of a boundary spectrum. I appreciate when the feeling of resentment arises in my own body, because it is often a sign that I wanted to set a boundary with others but didn't. The resentment is a helpful thread that leads me to a greater understanding of my own needs. Resentment can be an invitation to get to know yourself and your boundary needs better.

An invitation to explore: Take out your journal and do some writing to explore where you currently fall on the spectrum in external boundaries.

- *When I focus on my external boundary, what comes to mind is…*

- *I wall off or cut off from others when…*

- *I let down or drop my boundaries when…*

Now draw a spectrum line for yourself in your journal like this:

external boundary

rigid   porous

First, mark where you are now on the line, as best you can. Then ask yourself this question: *Wisest and kindest version of me, where would I like my home base to be?* Listen to the answer and then mark that point on the spectrum.

This will show you the difference between where you are and where you would like to be. It is a map that shows you what work to do. If you marked yourself on the rigid side of the boundary line and want to be a bit more in the middle, you might need to work on sharing your boundaries out loud in ways that are in your integrity. If you marked yourself on the porous end and want to move toward more firmness, then defining your actions and sticking to them will likely be your work.

Moving Forward

One of the hardest parts of boundary setting is experiencing the difficult feelings that can come up for you and others. In the next chapter, we dive into being with your feelings and the feelings of other people while using your psychological boundary to stay clear and integrated.

CHAPTER 3

Psychological Boundaries

Boundaries are the distance at which I can love both you and me simultaneously.

—Prentis Hemphill

The psychological boundary is an inner boundary that refers to the space and the difference between your mind and other people's minds. Our minds are both separate and connected. We each have our own personal journeys, histories, feelings, perceptions, brains, and needs. We also influence each other and share our energies, thoughts, and feelings with each other. Reinforcing the psychological boundary helps us hold these two truths simultaneously: we both are connected to others and are our own beings. This boundary is not meant to stop you from being affected by the feelings of others; being affected by each other is part of being human—it is normal and healthy. The psychological boundary will support your brain in helping you feel safer in all sorts of interactions. Holding awareness of your psychological boundary is especially helpful for the process of setting an external boundary; often, others will have a difficult reaction, and your psychological boundary will increase your experience of safety as you face their reaction.

Two skills are incredibly helpful in these interactions: the first is *discernment*, a process of determining when it helps to take in other people's feedback and when it doesn't. The second skill is *listening with acceptance*, which means letting other people have their feelings without trying to change them. In this chapter, you will develop these two skills and then interweave them with a bit of neurobiology to create a practice that will help your brain stay in an integrated state in the face of differences and difficult feelings.

Let's begin by looking at some of the feelings you experienced as you explored the six steps to setting an external boundary.

Exploring Feelings

As you worked with your six steps, did you notice that you were worried about hurting the other person? When you imagined sharing what is and is not okay for you, were you blaming yourself for hurting them or making them angry? Did you feel afraid to say what you wanted out loud? This may suggest you are hanging out on the porous end of the psychological boundary.

Alternatively, were you perhaps not worried about their feelings at all? This would align with a more rigid spot on the psychological boundary.

If you need help feeling more loving and connected to others, without feeling either invaded by them or burdened by them, then strengthening your psychological boundary will help. To start, it will help to understand a little more about the neurobiology of feelings.

What Feelings Tell You

You can listen to your brain in many ways. Some of the languages you will hear are movement, thought, sensation, image, and feeling. For now, let's focus on *feeling*: how a combined brew of everything you've ever learned from your history, plus your current aspirations, plus what's happening right now, comes to you in a little packet of information. We've named that packet of information "feelings," and it tells you what the world means to you moment to moment (Barrett 2017; Damasio 2021).

As previously discussed, your psychological floor has an area rug that knows how feelings work. That knowing has come from what you've experienced in your body and mind, interactions with others from your past and your present, and messages from the culture or cultures you live or were raised in. It's time to get curious about your current emotional knowings about feelings.

An invitation to explore: Use the following prompts to learn more about your feelings and your psychological floor. Write in your journal:

- *What are feelings, to me?*
- *What role do feelings play in my life and my decisions?*
- *When I have sad or hurt feelings, I hope others will respond by...*
- *When I feel anger, I hope others will respond by...*
- *When I have excitement or joy, I hope others will respond by...*
- *How did my parents or other close people express their feelings?*
- *When I think about how my parents responded to my feelings in childhood, I notice...*
- *When I think about how my partner or close friends respond to my feelings currently, I notice...*
- *When other people are angry around me, I usually...*
- *When other people laugh or show big excitement around me, I usually...*
- *When other people are sad or cry around me, I usually...*

Understanding your own psychological floor, or baseline, is important, because your experience is a combination of your history and past experiences and whatever information you are taking in from your body and the world around you right now. The prefrontal cortex of your brain is wired to simultaneously receive information from networks that process the here and now and networks that process everything you have ever known and learned (Eagleman 2021). So, your brain is reading the world of the present through the lens of your past.

In many ways, this is a convenient feature. Imagine not having this function! We would move through the world like newborn babies. We would have to relearn everything moment to moment: how to walk, what a chair is, the fact that on this planet stuff falls down. Our species wouldn't have made it at all.

You have to make sense of a hypercomplex world and know how to support yourself, getting needs and wants met while keeping yourself protected enough physically and emotionally. Thank goodness, your brain does all of that subconsciously.

Your brain assesses the resources and stimuli of the moment (how much you have slept, if you had a taxing day, that look your partner just gave you, your child whining) and simultaneously mixes this info with everything your psychological floor knows. This means accessing your emotional knowings about what each of these stimuli signifies, based on your previous experiences and your original emotional coding from early life. Based on your past experiences, your brain has a lexicon about what that kind of look means from your partner and what your child's whining may lead to. Voila! In less than a second, feelings will emerge. The feelings will help you make sense of what all this means to you right now, given everything you have ever known. And, crucially, these feelings help you and your body know what to do next (Badenoch 2018). We have often been told that we are thinking beings that sometimes feel, but the anatomical reality is that we are feeling beings that sometimes think (Damasio 1994).

How Emotions Help You Know What to Do

Your feelings help your brain know which muscles to send blood to in the next five seconds (Barrett 2017). Imagine for a moment that you're about to stand up, and notice what changes happen in your body. Your brain starts tensing muscles in your hips and ankles and increases your heart rate slightly, sending energy and blood to the places you will need them a couple of seconds from now. Your brain is preparing your body for action even though you haven't stood yet. Similarly, think of a time when someone gave you "that look," reminding you of something threatening or shaming in the past. Did your heart rate rise and adrenaline flood you, giving you tingles in your armpits and a flush of heat in your face? Or did you have a different physical response? These responses can happen in a lightning-flash of a second. In other words, emotions are functional experiences that help you make sense of the world and tell your body what to do next, before you even know how to think about what's happening (Menakem 2017).

This physiological arrangement of your neocortex also means that everything you've learned in the past—about how relationships work, who you are, what that tone of voice means, and what to expect when you state a need out loud—lives in you too (Siegel 2010a). Sometimes, what you have learned about how the social world works is excellent. Other times, stuff you have learned leaves you feeling scared, angry, or expecting to be hurt. When the expecting-to-be-hurt learning is cued, it can make you feel more guarded or vulnerable than you want to be. In such moments, it is likely that your brain will become unintegrated (Sapolsky 2017), which will lead you to act in old ways and be less able to stick with a boundary.

Take a breath and notice what is happening inside you. Do you sense that you're living out of everything you have known and learned? Do you perceive that your past is very much alive in your present? Mostly, we stay unaware of this process (Panksepp and Biven 2012). It happens at speeds that are too fast for the thinking-in-words part of our brains to keep up with: between one-quarter and one-fortieth of a second (Imms et al. 2021).

Now imagine another reader from a different part of the world or a different background reading these words. What the words mean to that person will be different from what they mean to you. Our differences as human beings are often the spice of life, and yet our differences can also be fuel for fear and frustration. Building your psychological boundary will help you feel less afraid and frustrated in the face of differences. Your psychological boundary will help you hold the fact that there are multiple ways of seeing the world, and that's okay—it's actually good. In Western culture, which demands either/or binaries of us, seeing and holding multiple truths can be a radical healing step.

Building Your Psychological Boundary

When building or reinforcing the psychological boundary in interactions with others, we use two skills: discernment and listening with acceptance. Discernment, or seeing clearly, helps you take in communication from others only if it is useful and healthy for you. With discernment, you keep out information (like other people's perceptions and words) that is not useful and, ultimately, not about you. By practicing discernment, you are protecting yourself psychologically and emotionally.

Listening with acceptance means witnessing and hearing someone else without trying to change their feelings or thoughts. As you practice listening with acceptance, you trust that the other person's feelings are important for them and are real; this allows you to be with other people's feelings without trying to change their feelings. This allows others to feel—and be—more psychologically safe in your presence. The psychological boundary protects your mind from the minds of others and their mind from yours.

I want you to hold this idea in your mind: *My feelings and other people's feelings are functional.* Feelings function to help each of us be more ourselves and know how to interact with the world in a way that serves us (Badenoch 2018). Your feelings help you, and other people's feelings help them. Feelings are a gift of being.

Let's look a little deeper at discernment.

Practicing Discernment

Practicing discernment means asking yourself these two questions: *Is it true or untrue?* and *Is it about me or not about me?* You ask yourself these questions whenever you are faced with information, interpretations, or feelings coming at you from another person. Continually practicing asking *Is it true?* and *Is it about me?* will allow you to be curious without taking things personally. If the answer to either of those questions is no, then this communication from the other person isn't personal. It is information about them, and, therefore, you do not need to take it into your heart or mind. This is the psychological boundary in action.

IS IT TRUE OR NOT TRUE?

Who gets to decide what is true and not true for you? You do. No one else can tell you for sure what is true for you and not true for you.

This position is empowering for some people, and it increases anxiety for others. One question I get asked a lot is "What if I get it wrong? What if I take it in and it's not true? Or what if I keep it out because I thought it wasn't true, but it was?" This is a common worry. I promise you this: you will get it wrong sometimes. You will, because that is what people do. Everyone makes mistakes, especially when they learn new things. When you do accidentally let in something that's not true, and you catch it, you can imagine pushing it out of your space, putting it on the other side of your boundary image (see exercise at end of this chapter).

You might keep something out that was true. You can make repairs with someone if it turns out you hurt them. We are all on a lifelong journey of learning and growing in our wisdom, connection, and humbleness, so making mistakes and making repairs is part of that journey. You don't have to be right; you get to learn and grow and become wiser as you find the ways that increase trust in yourself. The psychological boundary will be a practice in which you will get better and better at guessing what is true for you. At first, it will be slow, and then it gets faster and faster.

IS IT ABOUT YOU OR NOT ABOUT YOU?

The second half of discernment is asking yourself *Is it about me or not about me?* In the end, only when the information shared by another person is both true (as best you can tell) *and* about you will you let it in. Note: when someone is sharing information and uses "you" in their sentence, it does not mean they are necessarily sharing information about you. They might be sharing information about themselves. You keep from internalizing what they say, not to distance yourself from others but to feel more protected, so you don't take things personally, and this can stop you from becoming hurt and defensive. This will keep your brain in an integrated state and will allow you to lean in and become more curious and closer to others.

How close you want to be to others is up to you. For example, a stranger says something that could be insulting, but you don't let it in, because you determine it's not true and not about you. You're not hurt, and you may even feel good about protecting yourself psychologically. You're also probably not so curious about what that statement says about the stranger if you don't want to be close to them. However, if your partner or a friend says something that is not true and not about you, you are likely to stay very curious about what is going on for them, because you *do* want to be close with them. The level of your curiosity is going to be directly proportional to the closeness you want to have with the person who is speaking.

To help you explore this way of thinking, let's look at a boundary Matt is trying to set with his partner, Claire.

Process with Matt

Matt's wife, Claire, often becomes upset when Matt does things that feel "off" to her. She shows her upset feelings by raising her voice, telling Matt he doesn't care about her, and sometimes, in the heat of an argument, threatening divorce.

Sometimes this happens when Matt makes an error, such as coming home much later than planned or not doing something he has agreed to do. Other times it feels out of the blue to Matt—one time he brought home a cookbook he thought Claire would like, and she felt it was insulting. Matt knew the raised voice and harsh comments weren't okay with him, but asking Claire for things to be different hadn't changed anything.

"She tells me that she can't help how she feels, and that it's my fault—I'm insensitive. I do mess up. I was thirty minutes late the other day, so I get that I made her mad. I think it's my fault. I think I need to change, so she doesn't lash out. But I also want to tell her it's not okay to yell at me or threaten to divorce me when we fight. But I don't say anything, because it'll just make her more mad."

When it comes to setting boundaries with his wife and sticking to them, Matt needs help keeping his brain in an integrated state. Two things were adding to his distress: first, he thinks he is the sole cause of his wife's feelings, and second, he's experiencing her feelings as hurtful to him. Matt does two ineffective things in response: he tries to manage Claire's feelings, and he does not communicate his needs. Both of these have a high cost for him and for their relationship. Matt could strengthen his psychological boundaries by developing discernment and using the skill of listening with acceptance.

Working with the six steps to setting a boundary, Matt tried out defining his boundary action (step 2), and he made a guess at anticipating Claire's response (step 3).

"I could say, 'I want to know all about your feelings, but I can't listen when you are yelling. When that happens, I am going to leave the room, and I'll come back in fifteen minutes so that we can try again, because I do want to hear you.' But I know she will say, 'I just get mad when you're being insensitive. I don't yell. I am passionate, and this is just how I feel feelings. You are asking me not to be who I am.' Then I will be stuck." Matt looked tense as he imagined Claire's reaction. The tension is a clue that more protection would be helpful for Matt's brain, so we focused on building his psychological boundary. First, we looked together at discernment.

"Okay, Matt, let's slow that down and take this a step at a time," I recommended. "You hear Claire say, basically, 'You're the problem. You make me angry.' Is that true or not true for you? What is causing the anger? Be nuanced about it. What we want and what we've learned through our life influences feelings too."

"She wants me to do things her way. But that's not okay. I get it," he said. "So if I set a boundary, and speak up when I usually don't, I anticipate she will get mad about that. I am asking for a shift. I get that she would have some feelings about that, because she doesn't want to have to change the way she expresses herself. She'll also be mad that I am not okay with something she's doing, and thinking she might need to change, so that feeling is coming from her."

"Also, her family does this. They get loud and argue to get their way," he added. "So, it's not totally my fault that she's mad." Matt breathed out a long breath. Matt grew up in a family that blamed their feelings on each other most of the time; he'd long since learned to stay quiet, and not rock the boat. To think about feelings with more nuance—to realize he was not automatically responsible for *all* of someone else's upset—was a big shift for him.

"Good. The other thing you imagined her saying was that she doesn't yell, she's just passionate. Is that true or not true?"

"Oh, she yells, for sure. It's also true that she's passionate." He laughed.

"Good, so don't let the 'I don't yell' thing in, because that's not true. It is information about her and not about you. It sounds like the passionate thing is true, but it's not about you, so you can also let that be information about her and keep it out. And the last thing you were guessing she would say is that you do not want her to be who she is—is that true and is it about you?" I asked.

"No, I love who she is!" Matt was vehement. "I just want the yelling to stop. And it's totally on me that I haven't brought it up like this before now. I've been dealing with it by avoiding her," Matt realized.

"So this is true, yours to own and speak to: the way she expresses anger is hard for you; you do not want her to change who she is; and it took you too long to bring it up. Everything else is important information about the woman you love. Then, only holding what's yours, how would you answer her?" I asked.

"I would say, 'I am sorry I haven't said anything before now about what I need. I hide what I need from you, and that's not fair to you or us. I love you and I don't want to change who you are. But I need to take a break if yelling happens. I'm going to leave the room if you yell, because that's part of who I am. It doesn't mean I don't love you. It means I'm taking care of myself. Okay?'"

"Matt, that's a great answer," I said.

Matt smiled, "Yeah, if I said all that, she would understand, I think. We would feel closer. Unless she was having a hellish day, then who knows?"

"Well, no matter what happens on the other side of the line, your answer was true for you, and you shared yourself with her," I said. "I can't promise anything about what might happen in the other person. But you are supporting a more integrated brain state and keeping your psychological boundary—the boundary between her mind and your mind—strong while you talk with her."

"I think it'll go better on my end, regardless of what she does," Matt said. "And I don't think I can ever totally prevent her from yelling, so at least I have a plan when she does."

Can you see how not automatically taking in other people's feelings as totally true and about you can make difficult conversations easier and more collaborative? It helps if both people are doing this work. But even if others around you are not working on their psychological boundaries, you can work on yours. Be in charge of increasing your inner peace by protecting yourself and only taking in, or believing, what is important for your growth: what is true and what is about you. This process of discernment is an important foundation for your psychological safety.

In Matt's imagination of their potential exchange, Claire said Matt was at fault because he made her mad. This is a sticky point in many people's relationships. Do we actually cause other people's feelings? Are we responsible for causing their feelings?

One of the hardest things about being human is facing this fact: you have influence but no control. When you live and interact with others, everything you do influences the environment and, therefore, the people around you. You influence their thoughts and feelings, but unless you are doing something that's boundary violating (like stealing money from them or calling them a nasty name), you are not the *sole* cause of anyone's feelings. Feelings are complex and rooted in each person's history and neurobiology as well as their current response to their environment.

Are you ready to practice? Wherever you are in your journey with discernment is exactly where you should be right now. No judgment needed, just discovery.

An invitation to explore: Answer these questions as you explore discernment: the practice of only taking in what is both true and about you. Approach whatever you find with compassion and curiosity.

- How confident are you that you can tell what is true for you and not true for you? (If you like, use a scale of 1 to 7, where 1 is not at all confident and 7 is extremely confident.)

- How confident are you that you can tell what is about you and not about you? (If you like, use a scale of 1 to 7, where 1 is not at all confident and 7 is extremely confident.)

- In your growth, do you need to work on keeping more out or taking more in? If you are on the rigid side of the psychological boundary, taking in other people's feedback more will help you soften. If you are on the porous side of this boundary, taking in less of what others say and trusting your own mind more might be helpful.

Now, let's turn our attention to the second knowing of the psychological boundary, listening with acceptance.

Listening with Acceptance

When someone around you is experiencing a feeling, it is respectful to bear witness to that feeling with kindness and as much distance as is right for you—and not try to manage or control that feeling. This is the essence of listening with acceptance: listening and receiving others' feelings, without trying to exert your will over their emotions or asking them to change their feelings. Their feelings are part of their making sense of themselves and the world. Remember that everyone's feelings are generally functional. Your feelings are trying to help you; their feelings are trying to help them.

When you try to get others to feel and think differently, you are asking them to change themselves, which is often for your own benefit rather than theirs. Note that I am not talking about behavior here. Take Matt as an example. He doesn't try to change Claire's angry feeling or get her not to have that feeling, but he is saying he will move away from certain expressions of that feeling. Certain expressions of that anger are behaviors that are not okay with him, and he will act by increasing distance if they appear. He is saying what he will do, not what Claire should feel.

Ultimately, distinguishing between feelings and behavior can help you be kinder and closer to others. Anger is a feeling; yelling is a behavior. Judgment is a feeling or a thought; rolling the eyes is a behavior. Sometimes, behaviors from others are dangerous or hurtful. You can use the six steps to protect yourself in these circumstances. But most of the time, what other people are experiencing is not about you or dangerous to you. When you listen with acceptance to another's feelings and thoughts, you are witnessing them being themself, which is a gift. You can witness the other person's feelings as an expression of who they are, and also protect yourself from any hurtful behavior. Doing this will help you know how to respond to a situation with nuance and connection.

To really practice listening with acceptance, we have to remember that emotions are functional. Emotions function at a speed and frequency that outpaces our conscious thought many times over (Damasio 2021). Networks in our subcortical brains gather sensations from the body, messages from our senses, information from our conscious thoughts and current hopes and goals, and weave all of that together with anything that might be relevant from our past. In less than a second, an emotion occurs (Barrett 2017).

Think of emotions as one way your system is trying to understand the world, giving you high-speed data about what the stimuli happening around you mean to you in this moment of your life and what they might mean in your future (Dennis-Tiwary 2022). Each complex emotional experience tells you what this moment means and who you are in relation to that meaning.

When you have a feeling or a thought, this is you becoming yourself through time. And just as this is true for you, so it is for everyone you encounter. When you witness feelings and thoughts in others, rather than try to change their feelings and thoughts, you can just listen, recognize, validate, and accept what they are feeling. It may take work, but it is worth it. Acceptance doesn't mean you have to agree with the feelings or the thoughts. It just means you don't reject or try to change them.

The best way to make sure a feeling gets bigger, more stubborn, or more immovable is to try to get it to go away or be different. When another person perceives you as judging their feelings, excitatory neurotransmitters (like norepinephrine and acetylcholine), which actually increase the strength and intensity of the feelings, are activated in their subcortical brain, making them more upset (Gu et al. 2016). I believe there is innate wisdom in this: each feeling comes with a purpose, to help us move toward the more complete and coherent versions of ourselves, so we can navigate the world successfully. Yes, even the hardest feelings. Our emotions are moving us into the next moment of our becoming. If you or someone else tries to stop the feeling that is trying to do good for you, it makes sense that it would get bigger, so that it can keep working for you.

When you have this knowing in your psychological boundary, it will be easier to stay connected with others even when they have feelings that are difficult for you to be with. Let's turn back to Matt's concerns about his wife Claire's thoughts and feelings to see this play out.

Matt was working on his anticipation that when he told her his boundary, Claire would say he didn't accept her as she is.

"I don't want her to think that I want her to change who she is. I need her to know that I love her," Matt said.

"I get that it would feel way easier if she didn't think that way, but hold on a moment—are you sure that her feelings and thoughts are a problem? What if they are important? Like, what if her feeling uncomfortable with you wanting something different is an important part of Claire letting go?" I asked.

"What I am watching you do, Matt, is believe a story that this feeling in her is bad," I added. "Maybe it is, maybe it isn't. Have I told you the story of the farmer? I know the Taoist version of this one, but it's been around for ages in many different spiritual traditions."

I told the story: "Once there was a farmer who had one son and one horse. One day his paddock was unlocked, and the horse ran away. The villagers all came to offer their condolences. 'It's so terrible, it's so awful, you lost your only horse,' they said. 'Terrible, hmm, we'll see,' said the farmer. The next week his horse came back, bringing with him twenty wild stallions. Now the farmer had twenty-one horses in his paddock. And the villagers all came saying, 'Oh, how wonderful, you have horses to help you. It's a blessing, so wonderful.' And the farmer said, 'Wonderful. Hmm, we'll see.' The next week, his son was kicked by one of the horses, and his leg was broken. The villagers all came to say, 'How terrible, how tragic, your only son and his leg is broken.' The farmer said,

'Tragic. Hmm, we'll see,' and the next week the army came to recruit all the men of fighting age, but they did not take his son, because of the broken leg. The villagers came to say, 'What blessings, how wonderful,' and the farmer said, 'Wonderful. Hmm, we'll see.'"

"Her feelings might lead to something good, even if they are bad feelings?" Matt asked.

I replied, "What if her feeling stressed or upset leads to more honesty or change in how she talks? I don't know that you can have it both ways—that you stand up for yourself and she feels only pleasant things. She has to make sense of what's happening between you, and thinking and feeling hard things might be part of that. I guess I'd hate for you to shield her from that."

"I never thought of it like that. My family always said, 'Happy faces, everyone!'" Matt reflected.

"I wonder if it would be more connected for you to be kind in the face of hard feelings, but not to try to change them. Please keep your psychological boundary up with me, and only let this in if it feels true and helpful to you," I told him.

"It's a new way to think about it," he said.

"Think about it like this. She says, 'You want me to be someone I am not.' And then, you make up a story in your head, telling yourself, 'It's terrible that she thinks that, and if she keeps thinking that, then…'"

"'Then we aren't gonna make it,'" Matt filled in.

"Right. And then instead of being curious, you try to get her to change, because she's so wrong about you wanting her to change."

"Oh my God! I am so freaked out by all her feelings and thoughts, I do want her to change them, so I'll feel better. I do want her to change," Matt said.

"Right, but if you only let in what's true and about you, you stay protected. Then you can be curious about how her thoughts and feelings are important for her journey and not try to control her responses. This protects her psyche from yours, too."

"She complains that I don't hear her, don't take her seriously. I think this way might change that," Matt said.

Your acceptance of another person's feelings will likely feel supportive to them, while trying to change their feelings can land as disrespectful and painful, as if their feelings are not okay with you. Listening with acceptance allows you to be closer to people when they are feeling hard or unpleasant feelings. As you help them feel less alone with their feelings, it often will support internal shifts in the person you are listening to. That is, things can change without you working to help or change anything. The other person's feelings are much more likely to change if you validate and accept them than if you push for a different emotion.

Now you have explored the two ideas that will create your psychological boundary. Good work. If we embed your understanding of discernment and listening with acceptance into your psychological floor, these ideas will become part of your superhero-quick subcortical brain and help you stay in more integrated states, even in times of stress.

How Neural Networks Communicate

Neural networks help you understand the world quickly without having to relearn previously known information. This capacity is an incredible time saver created by nature (Kandel 2006). As discussed in chapter 1, neural networks develop patterns of activation over time, and the longer these patterns are in place, the more it will take to open the networks to let in new information. This means that neural networks can get stuck in time and hold onto the past in ways that aren't helpful. Luckily, our brains are a place of dynamic change: we can grow new neural networks and inscribe new patterns of wiring and firing (Eagleman 2021). Every neural network is constantly processing information and creating meanings, understandings, and predictions about how the world works.

The Mentalization Neural Network

A particular network that's key to the study of boundaries is called the *mentalization neural network*. This network refers to the many areas of the brain that combine information to create guesses about what is happening in the mind of another person (Luyten and Fonagy 2015). It is also the system in your brain that can tell the difference between you and others (Muscatell et al. 2012). It can differentiate between your mind and the minds of others with a processing speed as fast as one-twelfth of a second (Yordanova, Duffau, and Herbet 2017). This ability to differentiate between *me* and *them* is an absolutely critical feature, and one we draw on in boundary setting.

The mentalization neural network is mainly subcortical, although parts are in the prefrontal cortex and neocortex (Overwalle and Vandekerckhove 2013). It is the system in the brain that processes facial recognition, facial differentiation, and moral reasoning. It also receives much of its information from the center of the body (Luyten and Fonagy 2015). This means that the system in your brain that is guessing what is going on in the minds of others is listening to your heart and belly! This network speaks in image and metaphor better than in words (McGilchrist 2009).

The great news about all this is that if you speak to the mentalization neural network in its own way—with images—you can embed your psychological boundary in your psychological floor, making it a permanent part of your emotional and behavioral baseline that you can access with ease. With practice, the mentalization neural network will automatically process your psychological boundary for you and incorporate this boundary into your way of understanding things, making it much faster to keep you feeling protected and, therefore, in an integrated brain state from which you can respond.

Knowing the reality of this neurological wiring has led me to start guiding clients through a practice to discover a unique way of recalling their psychological boundary in a single image. I think about the word "image" broadly, encompassing picture, gesture, sound, metaphor, or even a word or phrase. If everything in you comes up with a word or words, you can simply float them in image form.

Your image or metaphor is unique to you. It might, at first, seem unrelated to boundaries at all. Trust yourself to provide the right image and be open to whatever comes, even if it seems strange. Be welcoming to whatever arises. Take a few moments to close your eyes and try it yourself.

PRACTICE: Find Your Boundary Image

You know that discernment is possible: you can take in what is true and about you and keep out what is not true and not about you. You know it is kind and respectful to bear witness to others' feelings and thoughts without trying to change them. Even if you are not great at it yet, you know it is possible to do it and can learn to do it better.

Now ask your heart and belly and all the space in your diaphragm to hold these two truths for you: discernment and listening with acceptance.

Next, ask your heart, belly, and center to show you an image that knows these two truths: *It is kind to bear witness (listen with acceptance), and there is no need to take in what is not true or yours (discernment, seeing clearly).*

Listen and wait. Be open to whatever image emerges, rather than trying to figure out the right image. Ask, listen, and wait. Close your eyes, and let an image arise in your mind. Give this as much time as you need. Then open your eyes.

An invitation to explore: Record in your journal the image that came to you in this practice. If you prefer, you can draw the image instead.

I have guided many people through the process of discovering the image for their boundary, and have yet to encounter an identical image. Themes that come up often are related to fences, walls, or water. Rivers, walls, waterfalls, bubbles, or hula hoops can surround a person. I have also heard these images, to name a few: a lion on the person's right side that has the essence of their old dog, monster truck tires, a tiny turquoise turtle hanging on a milk glass, a three-part gesture with the words "I'm okay, you're okay, it's okay," the word connection in neon orange floating in front of the person's face, and a translucent kangaroo, blinking. My point is this: your image comes to you from your inner world, like your dreams do, and anything you receive is good.

Matt found his image by following this practice.

"It's so weird, it feels like—the image that popped up in my mind is that it's my old G.I. Joes from when I was kid."

"Okay, I trust your system," I said. "Think about using your boundary with your wife. Picture her, but put the G.I. Joes in between you. You can see through them, and on the other side you see her."

"That's so weird. It feels calmer. Like, I trust her more?"

"Yeah, that's common. Does it feel like you don't have to manage her reaction as much?" I asked him.

"Exactly!" he said.

"Okay, try step 2 now. What would you say to her, with the G.I. Joes in between you?"

With his eyes closed, Matt said, "I want you to know that I should have said I was upset a long time ago. I think that's made this more painful for both of us and I am sorry. When you are angry with me, I do want to understand and listen to you. And when you are raising your voice or threatening divorce, it is not okay with me, and I can't listen the way I want. When that happens for me, I am going to take a thirty-minute break and then come back and try to talk with you again."

"How did that feel?" I asked him.

"Shaky, but better," Matt answered.

Now, recall something that has already happened in your life and imagine what it would be like to have your boundary image in that situation.

An invitation to explore: Think of a moment in your life when you wish you'd had a stronger psychological boundary. If you would like, you can choose a scenario that's medium or mild in stress level. Maybe you took in too much or tried to change another person's feelings. Perhaps you wanted to take in someone else's truth but went rigid and rejected it. Take your time bringing the interaction to mind, so you can be back in it a bit. Then write in your journal using these prompts:

- Remember the interaction. Where were you? What time of day was it? What did the other person look like? What was said or done?

- Go back to the beginning of that scene and imagine placing your boundary image between you and the other person. Make it so you can see through the image to them on the other side. Or think of sensing your boundary image between you and the other person.

- How do you feel toward the other person with your boundary image in place?

- How do you feel toward their feelings?

- Is what they said true or not true?

- Is what they said about you or not about you?

- How is your boundary holding up?

- What insights did you receive?

If your boundary held, you would likely feel a slight emotional shift: safer, more curious, or more compassionate to yourself and the other person. You have found your image.

If it isn't holding as well as you would like, go back to your heart and belly and ask, *What else could you do with this image that would help it be stronger and more flexible?* And wait until you see something new or perceive a shift in the original image. Then try journaling again. Continue until you find the image that gives you a perceptible emotional change that helps you feel more centered and self-trusting.

Often, when people do this practice over time, their image shifts or transforms as the subconscious system gets better and better at the work. If this happens for you, trust your system and go with the shift.

How to Change Your Brain

Now that you have your boundary image, I want to introduce another practice. One way your brain changes is through creating new neural networks. To do this, you are going to use the idea "skill, practice, state, and trait" to make big shifts in your brain and behavior over time (Siegel 2010b).

To break this idea down, when you are learning something brand new—a *skill*—if you *practice* it consistently for about three weeks, you will end up creating a new neural network: new patterns of connections in your brain that make that skill possible. This new neural network will be incorporated with other associated neural networks to form a *state*, which is a pattern of activity and connectivity in the brain that creates a whole way of being as long as that state is active. If you access that state purposefully and consistently over time, in about two to three years you will create *traits*, or make permanent shifts to your brain that are usually automatic and will not be consciously recalled.

Skill, practice, state, trait means that you can change the way you feel and act, what you believe, and the physical and electrical connections between neural networks in your brain. Then, the new state you've achieved becomes your brain's home base, and your old ways of feeling, acting, and experiencing the world will permanently shift.

Your creation and use of your boundary image is a brand-new skill. The more frequently and consistently you practice it by bringing your image to mind, and visualizing it between you and the world, the stronger a new state you will create. Remember, it only takes three to four weeks of repeating the practice to hone a new neural network. This network will become a part of your *in-relationship state*, the way you are in relationships. Then it will become a trait, an integral part of your personality and who you are.

PRACTICE: Use Your Boundary Image

Mentally place your boundary image between yourself and everything else in your world, whether it is a hard moment or not. Practice placing it between you and other people, you and dishes, you and the cat, you and the steering wheel, you and that stressful email. Just bring your image to mind as often as you can. This practice will usually take one to five seconds each time you do it. The more you practice, the more embedded this image and all the wisdom it represents will be for you, and the more accessible this new version of your in-relationship state will be for you.

You might be one of those folks who has a hard time with visualizing images. I am too. This will still work for you. Just remember a sense of the image that you found and put it between you and the world.

Remember the image, visualize it or sense it, and move on with your day. How often could you do this every day for the next three to four weeks? Ten times a day? How about twenty or fifty or a hundred? Take out your journal and make a commitment to yourself in writing: "I will practice remembering my image and placing it in between me and the world. I aim to do this..."

Your Psychological Boundary Spectrum

As we wrap up the psychological boundary chapter, let's revisit the rigid-porous spectrum and give you a chance to look at where you often land or hang out when it comes to your internal psychological boundary. Here's an easy way to tell. On the porous side of the psychological boundary, you will let in lots of thoughts and feelings from others, and you will want others to change what they think and feel. On the rigid side of the psychological boundary, you will let in very little from others, and you might think they are unpersuadable.

If your habit is to land on the porous side of the psychological boundary, you likely are easily affected by the moods, thoughts, and feelings of others. It may feel painful or scary when others think badly of you or when they are hurt by something you did. It may have been adaptive to be more porous in childhood: if you were in a family or a culture where reading people's feelings helped you stay more connected or safe; or if you were a person whose identity was marginalized, so you had to take in more information about the dominant culture and their feelings, to manage dangerous situations.

It is common for folks hanging out on the porous side of the psychological boundary spectrum to try quite hard to change others' thoughts and feelings until they learn to intentionally stop doing this. If you are on the porous end, you might get feedback from others that sounds like "I am allowed to feel what I feel!" or "Stop trying to get me to see it your way" or "Wow, don't be so sensitive." This is because you likely take in a lot from others and can be deeply hurt or scared by it. You may try to change what others are thinking and feeling to decrease all that hurt.

If you have a more rigid psychological boundary, you might find that you're not easily moved or shaken by feedback from others. You do not tend to take things personally, which can be both helpful and costly. You might not be easily rattled. You might also get the message from others that they feel unheard by you or that you are hard to work with because you have trouble taking in feedback. They may say, "You don't care what I feel and think" or "All you need is yourself—why am I here?" You might find it hard to understand what others are feeling and have trouble making sense of their perspectives, feelings, and thoughts, even when they share them in detail. If you are on this end of the psychological boundaries spectrum, you may think of other people's feelings as dramatic, ridiculous, or overblown.

Hanging out at the rigid side of the psychological boundary spectrum can feel lonely. Relationships may feel burdensome. You might cut yourself off emotionally from other people, so others can have a hard time knowing or guessing what you are feeling.

There are times when going more rigid psychologically is ideal, like if your child is having a tantrum and calling you names or if someone posts something cruel on social media. Not letting it deeply affect you is a helpful strategy; it will help you avoid being harsh with your child or internalizing hurt you don't deserve. Likewise, it might be a good idea not to let more feelings and thoughts in if you are in a tense moment with a partner or close friend, and they are in a space of communicating with harshness. Staying on the rigid side can also be a healthy act of resistance for those who live in bodies that are frequently marginalized and shamed, so you do not take oppressive messages in.

There are also times when going more porous is helpful. For example, when listening to a friend share a different view of how life feels for them, moving to the porous end of the boundary (accepting a lot more information, believing their perspective is real and valid, letting it move you) might increase your connection. If you are having trouble understanding someone, putting your own thoughts and feelings to one side for a moment to focus on theirs, and trying to see yourself in their shoes, can help you increase empathy and compassion.

You are the best judge of whether spending more time on the rigid or porous side of this boundary is best for you. When you are considering where you are on the psychological boundary spectrum now and where you want to be, the important thing is to wonder about what you want for yourself, not what others might think a "healthy boundary" is. Healthy is not in the middle of the spectrum; healthy is what is right for you culturally and personally with flexibility in response to different situations.

An invitation to explore: Take out your journal and do some writing to explore where you currently fall on the psychological boundary spectrum.

- *When I focus on my psychological boundary, what comes to mind is...*

- *I go rigid when...*

- *I go porous when...*

Now draw a spectrum line for yourself in your journal, like this:

psychological boundary

rigid   porous

First mark where you are now on the spectrum. Then ask yourself, *Wisest and kindest version of me, where would I like my home base to be?* Mark that place on the spectrum. If you marked yourself on the rigid end and would like to move toward the porous end, then you will want to work on your psychological boundary image letting more in. Conversely, if you marked yourself on the porous end and would like to move toward the rigid end, you will want to work on your boundary image keeping more out.

Moving Forward

The next chapter will introduce the containing boundary. This internal boundary gives you a way to pause in hard moments and keep your behaviors and speech aligned with who you want to be.

CHAPTER 4

Containing Boundaries

Self-compassion is not the same as being easy on ourselves. It's a way of nurturing ourselves so that we can reach our full potential.

—Kristin Neff

In the heat of the moment, all of us can act in ways we later regret. The containing boundary helps us choose our actions rather than act on impulse or high emotion. This is the inner work that will support you to align your actions and words with your integrity and your relational hopes. You have influence on others, so it benefits you to use your influence with choice, empowerment, and consideration.

The containing boundary helps you say what you need to say while also being kind and staying in your integrity, not acting in ways you don't want to. The containing boundary is about saying only what you need to say and no more, and being respectful with how you say what you say and do what you do. The primary practice of the containing boundary is putting a pause between what you think and feel and what you say and do.

Owning Your Influence

The psychological boundary work in the last chapter helped you integrate the reality that you do not control the feelings of others and it can hurt to try. In this chapter, you will work on the awareness that although you do not control others, you do influence them—and so it's important that your behavior aligns with your values. You will examine the practice of adding a pause between what you feel and what you say or do and using a physical gesture to support yourself. You will choose key words to rapidly remind yourself of your values. These tools weave together to create your containing boundary. Think of a flowerpot: it contains the soil and the plant so that they stay in place; the soil does not spill out everywhere, and the plant remains upright.

One of the first skills we lose in an unintegrated brain state is the ability to pause between feeling and doing (Siegel 2020). When people feel concerned that something is about to go wrong, their brain becomes unintegrated to add speed. The added speed is great if you are being physically threatened but costly in difficult emotional interactions. When we lose the ability to pause, emotions run our lives by pulling up old maps from our psychological floors about how to act. This is especially hard news if we are trying to make boundaries that stick, because if our brains stay in an unintegrated state, then we are more likely to do what we have always done rather than make the shift that we want.

In this unintegrated brain state, we are likely to defend ourselves by moving to whichever end of the rigid–porous boundary spectrum we are accustomed to. If we become too porous, we might speak harshly or act outside of our integrity, by name-calling, blaming, insulting, or saying harsh rejecting words. We might flex or drop our boundary and agree to someone else's wishes and then regret it. If we become too rigid, we might not speak up for ourselves in the first place or might turn away from the conversation and shut down. All of these can create difficult feelings and feedback loops. None of these are ideal, so we need to practice.

Wherever you are in your current boundary-setting skills, adding a pause between what you feel and what you do will help tremendously.

The Neurobiology of Pausing

When you put in a pause and soothe the feelings that are arising, so they do not take control of you, you are creating an alternate path to the reactivity that can arise in relationships. This pause increases the connection between your prefrontal cortex, where emotional regulation and moral reasoning are processed (Siegel 2020), and your subcortical mind of emotions and the knowings of your psychological floor (Badenoch 2018). In reality, your subcortical layer processes your emotional knowings from the past and current feelings much faster than your neocortex layer integrates information and produces your thoughts and words (Kahneman 2011). We cannot change this speed difference, much though we might want to.

Neurobiology helps us understand that the containing boundary is exercised by running electricity in the pathways between your prefrontal cortex (a part of your neocortex) and your subcortical mind (Sapolsky 2017). The neocortex is made up of layers of neurons that are arranged into columns. Each column is made up of six layers (Siegel 2020), and there are about 200 million cortical mini-columns (Johansson and Lansner 2007). The top two layers of neurons in the neocortex receive their information from systems in the brain that are living in memory, what has been previously learned and discovered in your life's journey. The bottom two layers of neurons in the neocortex get their information from neural networks that process the stimuli in the present moment. When the bottom two layers and the top two layers of brain cells combine their information in the middle two layers, the result is what this moment looks and feels like to you (Siegel 2020). In fact, the top two layers (from your history) have much more influence on your present experience than the bottom two layers (Siegel 2020). That's why I say your brain wears history-colored glasses; your history colors all you see.

You cannot keep your subcortical brain from producing the feelings it does. Feelings are essential to making sense of the world, and your mind depends on them to survive (Damasio 1994, 2021). However, as we know that feelings are produced much faster than thoughts, it is helpful to build a pausing practice into your experience. That way, you can integrate your slower, more responsive mind and values with your wise and functional feelings before acting and responding.

The prefrontal cortex can synthesize and integrate everything you are experiencing. It is the part of the brain that regulates and that can witness your thoughts, feelings, and behaviors (Siegel 2010a). When your witnessing mind is kind toward the rest of you and you feel compassion toward yourself, it will send signals that release calming neurotransmitters in your subcortical brain (Longe et al. 2010).

Inside the pause, you will have the chance to stop using words and actions that are outside of your integrity. Then you can do the hard work of choosing actions that simultaneously protect and support you and treat others well, if you wish to. Without this pause, you might find yourself at the mercy of emotional storms. Of course, you are not in an emotional storm all the time (even if sometimes it feels that way), so rest assured, your brain already has some ability to soothe and shift. You can help it do this more effectively by pausing to shift and self-soothe on purpose and with kindness.

Developing the Pause

The primary task of the containing boundary is developing a pause between what you feel and what you do. I can't tell you how long to pause: in some situations, ten seconds is enough; in other situations, ten minutes, ten hours, or ten days may be needed. You will have to feel out how long a pause you need to ground and support yourself or find supportive community to help you, when faced with a challenging communication or situation. The fact of the pause is the crucial thing.

Within the pause, you will do two things: soothe your feelings with a compassionate gesture and remind yourself of your values—your personal integrity and your relational hopes—with one or two words. You do this so that your behavior is something you can be proud of. The pause helps you stop in the heat of the moment and pull your values system into focus. You can think of it in shorthand: Pause + Compassion Gesture + Values Words = Containing Boundary.

Do you know your own values? Do you know what you believe and what kind of person you would like to be? I find that most values fall into two categories: personal integrity and relational intentions. *Personal integrity values* are the kind of person you want to be in the world. *Relational intention values* are who you want to be in relation to other people; how you want to be nourished by the relationships you have; and how you hope to nourish others. Of course, these two kinds of values are deeply connected.

It can be hard to remember our values if we have a long list of them. But with a short list of one or two words, it can be a quick way to keep yourself on track. These are key words you will reach for when creating your pause.

PRACTICE: Find Your Personal Integrity Key Word

When you think of the best version of yourself, what do you see? How would you describe yourself when the things you do and the words you say are generally in alignment? This is not about perfection—we can all let that go. What you're looking for is the nature of your values around personal integrity and a key word to describe those values. For example, you might look at your best self and think, *brave, bold, calm in the face of hard stuff, inspiring, and creative*. Then as you pause and feel out each of those words, you might realize that for you each one requires one key element: *courage*. That is your integrity key word.

Use these questions to find a personal integrity key word for yourself.

- Think of the best version of yourself, the person you most deeply wish and aim to be. Now write down five words to describe the person you see.

- Find one word that encompasses all five of those words, or an umbrella term under which all the others would fit.

- How do you feel as you try on this word as a core value? Does it fit for you?

If it fits, this is your key word for personal integrity, which you will use as part of your containing boundary.

Now let's find a word to anchor your relational values and hopes for connection. Humans thrive on our interconnectedness. Though some of us may lean more introverted and others more extroverted, some may like a few deep connections while others prefer light-hearted folly in large groups, people need people. Researchers have found that we feel less stress, imagine difficult tasks to be easier, heal more quickly, and have better mental health overall when we connect with others (Murthy 2020).

What connection with another feels like and who you want to be in your relationships is unique to you. Finding a word or two that encompasses your desired way of showing up in relationships is an important part of your containing boundary. It will help you quickly identify what behaviors are in alignment with your relational intentions and values.

PRACTICE: Find Your Relational Intentions Key Word

Think of the ideal version of you in three different relationship spaces. One space is with someone you are close to, like a partner or friend; the second one is with someone who is dependent on you, even for a brief time, such as a child or an animal or even a person you are helping; the third is a moment with a stranger. Then imagine you take a snapshot of yourself showing up in each of those three relational spaces in a way that feels fulfilling and that you can be proud of. And imagine laying those snapshots out so you can look at all three of those moments at once and consider what they might have in common.

Use these questions to find a key relational intentions value word for yourself. You may want to write in your journal.

- Based on what you see in the snapshots, how do you want to be when you connect with others?

- Find five words to describe the person in the three snapshots.

- Now find one word that encompasses all five of those words.

- Describe one moment when your thoughts and behavior in relating to others matched that word.

- How do you feel as you try on this word as a core value? Does it fit for you?

Continue to work on finding the words for your values key words: one for personal integrity and one for your relational intentions. Once you have discovered both, you can use these key words inside your pause to check out the actions you take.

Here is how this worked for Veda and Amir.

Process with Veda and Amir

Veda and Amir are a married couple with two children, Omar and Meera, ages three and five. Veda was working through a boundary with the kids, around their being destructive with the family's furniture. I repeated back the plans Veda had made about communicating with them.

"So, you are going to say to Omar, 'I see you jumping on the couch. That is not okay with me. If you can't stop your body from jumping, I will pick you up and help you to stop.' So even though there are lots of ways they might damage the furniture, you can lean into this formula we've created: 'I see you doing this. That's not okay. I hope you stop, and if you can't, I will help you stop.' Did I get that right?" I asked.

"Yes," said Veda, "and that part feels okay, not too hard. I think the formula is good for me. But what they do next could be a problem. I can see how they might keep going—Meera might roll her eyes. They don't listen to me. I see red when this happens. It is so disrespectful. I get very, very mad. And then I get mad at you," she turned to Amir, "because I want you to step in and make them respect me. But you don't; you go quiet instead. Then I am saying mean things. I might walk out of the room, slam the bedroom door. I am not okay in this kind of moment."

"And I do not support you well," Amir added. "I see that."

As Veda breathed deeply to calm herself and held Amir's hand, I thought she could be helped by bringing a pause to that hard moment of anger, so I offered a containing boundary practice. I explained the concepts, and then we jumped into the exercises to help her find her two value words.

"If you think about the wisest and most authentic version of yourself, who you want and aspire to be, what image do you see?" I asked Veda.

With her eyes closed, she said, "I am standing tall and wearing my teal sari and smiling and full of peace."

"Now, can you list four or five words or short phrases that would describe the woman you see?" I asked.

"I am strong, certain, confident, self-assured…I know my mind," Veda said, opening her eyes.

"Good, so look at that list." I passed her a piece of paper with those words on it. "Is there a single word that could encompass all these?"

"Quiet confidence," Veda said. "It must be both, because my brother is confident but arrogant, and I don't want that. Oh, 'quiet confidence' is right, for sure. My heart relaxes and beats strong at the same time. But you said only one word."

"Do it your way. Your way will always be better for you," I said.

She smiled. "'Quiet confidence,' then."

"So that's your phrase that will help you recall your personal integrity. Now let's find your relational intention word. Picture yourself with Amir in a moment when you feel connected and great about yourself."

"Yes, I have one," she said.

"Good, now picture yourself with Omar and Meera in a moment when you are showing up as the kind of mother you want to be."

Veda smiled and nodded.

"Good," I said, "Now picture a moment with a stranger in which you felt you were showing up well. When you have that, I want you to put your three pictures side-by-side in your mind's eye and then ask yourself, what do all three of those images have in common?"

"Well, this is strange," she said. "At first, I thought it was kindness, but it's not. In those moments, I have faith in them. I trust that they are doing things in a way that works for them. Then I do not have to fix anything, because they are doing okay. When I have faith, the pressure is off of me a bit," Veda said.

"Great," I said, "So now you have your values key words: 'quiet confidence' and 'faith.' Now let's add in some self-compassion, because compassion makes change happen more consistently than inner willpower or judgment."

Amir cut in, "Veda, I understand. All we grew up with tells us that if children push back, this should make us so angry. It makes me angry too. I shut down because that is what I saw; you get loud because this is what you saw." He put his hand over hers gently.

Veda looked at him and squeezed his hand. "This is understanding and compassion," she told me.

"Is there a gesture or a small movement you could do, Veda, that would remind you of this compassion?" I asked her.

"It is this." She gently put one of her hands over her other hand, like the gesture her husband had just done with her.

"So, you can put one hand over the other gently and say to yourself the words *faith* and *quiet confidence*. This reminds you with compassion of who you are at your core," I offered.

The Power of Self-Compassion

Your brain is soothed internally by compassion, not pressure, willpower, or emotion suppression (Neff 2011). Your neocortex can soothe your subcortical system when you direct compassionate thoughts and feelings toward yourself. Alternatively, you can really rile yourself up with judgments or attempts to force yourself to feel differently, both of which greatly stress your brain. A stressed brain is a brain with less integration.

If you use harsh words, unkind thoughts toward yourself, or force of will to create the pause between what you feel and what you do, the result will likely be a more powerful activation of the subcortical brain, in which your feelings become even more reactive, because you have added more that needs to be regulated. This may work well in the short run but usually leads in the long run to less of a pause between what you feel and what you do, as the subcortical brain gets energized and more distressed and you exert more pressure to control it.

If, on the other hand, you create a pause from the prefrontal cortex using your values key words and a self-compassion gesture, the pause can involve the regulating influences from that part of the brain: self-love, self-care, clear witnessing of yourself and your mind, and your moral compass.

Again, emotions are essential to understanding the world and are highly functional, so it wouldn't be wise to get rid of them. Even if you could, it is biologically impossible. Given the facts, you have a choice. If you ignore your feelings, push them away, or try to suppress them, then your emotions will run your behavior without your awareness. If, on the other hand, you accept that your feelings are useful to you and are here to stay, and you create a pause inside of yourself, you can develop a relationship with your feelings, listen to them, learn to love and welcome them, and ultimately soothe them.

Self-compassion activates gamma-aminobutyric acid (GABA), an inhibitory neurotransmitter, in your subcortical brain, particularly to the areas that process fear and pain (Stevens, Gauthier-Braham, and Bush 2018). GABA soothes your lower brain, creating the pause needed for you to do an internal boundary, if needed, and to choose your actions and responses intentionally.

PRACTICE: Find Your Self-Compassion Gesture

The goal is to find a gesture to do with your body, in real time, to remind yourself to pause at the moment when you would typically do a problematic behavior without thinking. The gesture will hold the intention of compassion. The part of your brain that will complete the movement, the basal ganglia, is a system that operates very quickly. It holds both the movement itself and the emotional intentions behind the movement at subcortical brain speeds. This system intertwines with your emotional system and can offer soothing directly without connecting through the slower neocortex.

To give you an idea of what this might look like, here are some gesture practices I have seen over the years. Steve places his hand on his stomach and says to himself, *You matter.* I put my hand on my heart and say to myself, *Courage and kindness*. Cole puts his hand on his heart and silently repeats the word *Goonies*. Melissa wiggles her fingers and says to herself, *You are magic*. Steph runs her fingernail on the seam of her jeans and tells herself, *Art and curiosity*. Mateo clasps his hands together and thinks, *Remember yourself and love*.

For you, the gesture might need to be bold and dramatic, or it might need to be tender, soft, or subtle. Trust yourself to find the thing that will work for you.

- Think about the behavior you want to change. Bring to your mind's eye the two words representing your personal integrity and your relational integrity.

- Greet all of these elements with compassion.

- Ask yourself, *Is there a movement that can remind me that I am good inside and facing a hard situation, like all people have to?*

- Try the gesture out. Do it with your body a few times. Imagine doing it in times of stress.

- Now make an agreement with yourself: *My commitment to myself is to practice this gesture…*

For another way to practice, go back into moments in the past and imagine the scene, but this time add the gesture, noting what it feels like to give compassion to yourself.

Just like Veda was practicing, you can put it all together and try using your gesture and key words. Try them in moments that feel positive or neutral, just to practice and remind yourself of who you are. You can also imagine doing them inside your work with the six steps. For many folks, the gesture and key words become part of the soothing plan in the fifth step. Containing boundary work is also helpful to do anytime in life, even when you are not setting a boundary. You have influence in many situations, and you can choose to use your influence in alignment with your personal integrity. So use your compassion gesture and value key words whenever you want to give compassion to yourself while remembering the values you want to stick to.

If you tend to move behind a wall or disconnect when you are under stress, the containing boundary can help you as well. If you notice this is happening, use your gesture and your words to help yourself pause and see if sharing more of yourself and your truth would align with your relational intentions and personal integrity. Then take a breath and move into more connection, sharing, or asserting yourself, whatever the situation may call for.

An invitation to explore: Think of a boundary you would like to set or one that has gone badly in the past. Take yourself through the six steps to setting an external boundary, but pause when you get to step 4, where you anticipate your own reactions. Expand your self-reflection there.

- What are the feelings and sensations you usually have at this moment?

- What behaviors might you usually do?

- How is that behavior trying to help you?

- Try on the thought *That behavior is not all of me.* What do you feel when thinking this thought?

- Compare the behavior to your two values key words. Do they match?

- What is a possible behavior that would match your values key words and also uphold the boundary you are setting?

- Slow yourself down, take a breath, and use your compassion gesture to add a pause.

- Go through the six steps in your mind again, but this time use your compassion gesture and values key words in step 5 for your self-soothing plan.

How was that for you?

Practice your self-compassion gesture, and when you do, remember to offer yourself love and care, and remember your values key words. Remind yourself that frequent action will make this a brand-new neural network for you. No matter what else happens, offering compassion with a gesture toward yourself will help you create the pause you will need to stick to your boundaries, even in emotionally intense situations. As you practice your psychological and containing boundaries, holding your external boundaries will get easier. It might not feel comfortable, but it will be easier to do the hard thing: keep your boundary.

Sometimes, the practice that will help us grow the most is to stay with a situation through difficult feelings. At other times, we need a bigger pause—a time-out—a time to breathe and reconnect with ourselves away from the situation. It is kind to let the other person know that we are taking a time-out, so they understand and don't feel we have simply left the interaction or abandoned them with it.

PRACTICE: Take a Time-Out

During moments when you are too riled up and distressed to do something different, it is great to give yourself a time-out. Whether you live with others or are communicating with people remotely, it can be helpful to let them know about your time-outs both before and when you take them. During your time-out, you give yourself some time, love yourself like crazy within that time, and then reengage in a way that aligns with your values.

To take a time-out, leave the interaction, if possible. Let the person you are with know that you are taking a time-out. Plan on being away from the situation for twenty minutes, or more if you need more time. There are many ways to take a time-out: take a walk, or go into a different room, or put on headphones if the space you're in together is small and you can't leave. If you're using technology, put the phone on silent. Do not text or call the person. Give your body and brain a real break.

Inside the time-out, breathe and bring some light and air in. Remember that what is happening right now is not all of you. Offer yourself deep kindness and love. Let yourself know that you are not alone, we all have moments like this, and they are tough. Compassion will help soothe the difficult feelings. Take some time to wonder about what is best for you next. Do you have a need or hope, or do you want to do something next that aligns with your two values key words? Make a plan for yourself. Practice your compassion gesture and soothe yourself. When you feel back in your integrity and integrated, then rejoin the interaction and reconnect with the person or people you took space from.

The containing boundary is used to build trust and safety within yourself. The more you show up in your integrity, the more you are compassionate with yourself. The more you show up in relationships in a way that is authentic and meaningful to you, the more you will trust in yourself. You can be your own best friend and biggest support system. I invite you to use the containing boundary practice to put the feelings of loving and supporting yourself into action.

Your Containing Boundary Spectrum

Let's take a moment to explore where you hang out on the containing boundary spectrum, and which direction you'd like to move in.

In a moment of porousness in the containing boundary, you will let out more, in the form of more words and more actions. In a moment of rigidness in the containing boundary, you will let out less; you will say less and do less.

If you spend lots of time on the porous side of the containing boundary, you probably express a lot. You might make friends easily. You might also tend to share more about your personal life than you mean to or offer people advice without prompting. You might get feedback from people you are close to that you are "too much." You might act outside of your integrity when you are upset. You might feel full of fury or hurt in one moment, and act out of those feelings, then regret it the next day. For folks on the porous end of the containing boundary, there is often both the feeling that what we do in upset moments may be outside of our value system and the feeling that others pushed us to this behavior and that our needs should be met. It is normal to have a bit of self-justification on this end of the containing boundary spectrum.

If you are on the rigid side more often, you will likely say too little. In fact, you might have difficulty knowing what is and is not okay with you and defining an action that would support your needs and safety. You might even go through the six steps in your mind but then not say anything out loud. Many folks I have worked with will say things like, "Why would I bother setting a boundary? No one will listen to me anyway..." or "People are ridiculous. I'd rather not deal with them." This can lead to withdrawal or walling off rather than boundary setting. If you tend toward this end of the spectrum, you may have received feedback that you seem shut down or unreachable. You might even have trouble getting to know yourself. In a conflict, you might walk out of the house without speaking; you might ignore calls and text messages, no matter how frantic they are. If things become overwhelming, you might ghost someone.

People who find themselves on either end of this spectrum often have a hard time apologizing. That's because on the rigid side, there's a tendency to not speak up about emotional truths, and on the porous side, there's a tendency to justify behavior, giving all the reasons why you did something rather than simply apologizing.

As you explore your internal world, remember, there is nothing wrong with you. Your containing boundary home base is due to modeling, feedback, and adapting to all the landscapes of your history and ancestry. Many boys have gotten feedback to be fairly rigid about how they share feelings and porous in how they go after what they want, whereas many girls have gotten feedback that guides them to be porous in sharing emotions and more rigid in asserting what they want. Wherever you land on this spectrum, you had a lot of help, so be curious and kind with yourself as you explore where you are and how you got there.

No one can tell you what is right for you as a home-base spot on the containing boundary spectrum; there are good reasons to land anywhere on this spectrum. It is also helpful to be able to flex from that spot as the situation calls for.

Your psychological floor is filled with adaptations because of various things you experienced. Your feelings are trying to help you increase your safety and well-being. You are getting to know your inner landscape so that building your pause between feeling and doing will be easier.

So without judgment, let's explore where you have been and where you want to go on this spectrum.

Invitation to explore: Take out your journal and do some writing about where you currently fall on the containing boundary spectrum.

- *When I focus on my containing boundary, what comes to mind is...*

- *I go rigid when...*

- *I go porous when...*

Now draw a spectrum line for yourself in your journal, like this:

containing boundary

rigid   porous

First, mark where you are now. Then ask yourself, *Wisest and kindest version of me, where would I like my home base to be?* Then mark that spot.

Moving Forward

Now that you have your psychological and containing boundaries in place and are practicing them, setting boundaries with others will get easier.

There is one more system that can trip you up in your boundary work, and it's located in your brain's physical safety system. The next chapter will introduce the ways that the lowest part of your brain, your brain stem, helps you assess your physical wellness and safety. If you feel scared in your body when setting and sticking to boundaries, this next chapter will help. We'll look at how protected and empowered you feel, and you will learn skills to support yourself as you create boundaries with others and live in alignment with your deepest values.

CHAPTER 5

Physical Boundaries

And there was a new voice, which you slowly recognized as your own, that kept you company as you strode deeper and deeper into the world, determined to do the only thing you could do— determined to save the only life you could save.

—Mary Oliver

Physical boundaries are your ability to experience your physical body as safe when you are relatively safe, to protect your physical well-being, and to create more safety when needed.

In one way of seeing it, your physical boundary is the edge where you end and the world begins. You do not need to do anything for this boundary to exist. Look down at your hand and arm right now. Notice that you have an edge that separates you from the air and other people. In this sense, your physical boundary is real and present with you all the time.

Your ability to protect and support your physical boundary is sometimes limited. With boundary work, you add protection rather than guarantee safety, because there is no absolute guarantee. I want to support your ability to repair your physical boundary if you need to and support your empowerment to take actions to increase your safety when you need to and can.

Your Safety System

Look around your space right now and notice if the space around your body is settled, protected, safe enough, and maybe even pleasant. Notice what happens to your breath as you take in your safety. Your brain's safety system is tracking your body and environment in this very moment to make sure you are safe enough. This system is largely located in the brain stem at the base of your skull. It helps out with many automatic functions such as keeping your heart beating and regulating breathing and sleep. It also assesses the current amount of safety you are experiencing. It makes this assessment about every one-quarter of a second! If it guesses you are in danger, it supports your body's defensive responses; if it guesses you are fairly safe, it supports your body's rest, calm, and social bonding responses (Porges 2011).

If your brain stem isn't perceiving physical safety, it is hard for the rest of your system to engage with others in an integrated and flexible way. In some ways, setting boundaries that stick starts with recognizing that your body is safe enough when it actually is. There are many simple ways to support your brain stem in sensing your body's empowerment and protection.

Before we get into those tools, I want to say that I know a lot can happen in this world—there are many things outside of your control that might hurt or invade your physical boundaries. When this happens, it is never your fault. No amount of physical boundary work can fully protect us from dangerous people, car wrecks, surgery, racism, homophobia, misogyny, other societal oppressions, natural disasters, or accidents. Boundary work can, however, help repair a felt sense of physical safety if your boundaries have been injured by events in your life. Boundary work can also help your brain stem register deeper interpersonal safety and will support your ability to stay longer in integrated brain states.

Communicating with the Brain Stem

Talking to your brain stem is an interesting task, because your brain stem does not speak English, Spanish, Mandarin, Swahili, or any other verbal language. Your brain stem speaks the languages of sensation, sensate input (sight, taste, sound, smell, touch), and movement. When you want your brain stem to hear you, you will have to speak so that it can understand (Levine 2015). That means you are going to be talking through your body. You will use sensations, your senses, and movement to talk to your brain stem.

As everyone has an individual experience when it comes to being with their bodies and sensations, I encourage you to honor your wisdom when it comes to how fast and deep to go with any exercise in this chapter. I also want to note that it is normal for those who have experienced trauma to become numb to their bodies or be easily overwhelmed by body sensation. If you have been through significant trauma at any age, it may be helpful to do these exercises with a trauma-informed therapist.

Try this brief exercise to process the fact that your physical boundary is real: it exists without any work on your part. In this exercise we will use your arm, but if exploring with your arm does not work for you, feel free to do it with any other part of your body that you can see, like your knee, toe, or pinky finger.

PRACTICE: Find Your Edges

Look at your arm, then shift your focus to the air just outside of your arm. Now, look at your arm again and say this out loud: "This is my arm. It is a part of my body. It is a part of me." Pause and notice whatever happens when you hear those words while you look at your arm. Then shift your gaze to the air outside your arm. "That is the air, which is not part of my body. It is part of the world around me." Then again move your gaze to your arm and repeat the words, "This is my arm. It is a part of my body. It is a part of me." Then move your gaze to the air. "That is the air, which is not part of my body. It is part of the world around me."

Each time, notice whatever sensations, emotions, or thoughts come. Let yourself go back and forth as many times as feels right. Then let your gaze fall on the edge of your arm, right where it meets the air. Feel the contact between you and the world. When you feel the edge of yourself touching the world, try these words: "Now my edge is touching the world, and in this moment that is okay." Track whatever thoughts, feelings, images, or sensations come as you bring the safety of your own edge into your awareness.

All of us are exposed to a consumer culture and media influences that teach us to feel dissatisfied with our bodies and to buy things to "improve" our bodies and appearance. Some people learned early on not to hold themselves and their own bodies in warm regard, and some people have received messages about not having a right to protect their own bodies.

Physical Boundary Influences

If there was a lot of judgment or criticism in your home, if you witnessed a parent not being able to protect their body, or if you were the target of boundary violations, you may need to build a new relationship with your physical body based in gratitude and connection. Likewise, you may need to build this relationship if your parents offered very little touch or consideration of how you were feeling. If you were taught to dislike yourself, starting with listening, respecting, and protecting your physical boundaries is a great way to shift toward self-appreciation.

I want you to get to know your what your body likes. Are you a person who likes more physical contact, or are you a person who feels better when you do not touch others and they don't touch you? There is no one "right" way to be. Health is honoring and living authentically for yourself, with the flexibility to shift when you need to.

Do you consider yourself more or less sensitive than others? People who are more sensitive feel big sensations in their bodies, which can lead to the world around them feeling intrusive or overstimulating. Other people are far less easily stimulated by their environment. There are great gifts in either way of experiencing the world.

Again, what you know about what kind of touch is okay and not okay for you is deeply influenced by your history. You might have been told explicitly or implicitly not to expect comforting touch. You might not have been able or allowed to protect your body when you were growing up. We all learned rules from family and peer interactions, and from our own cultures and dominant cultures that surrounded us. Luckily, we now get to rewrite some rules.

Our Bodies Inside Our Societies

It's important to acknowledge that social and cultural differences matter in boundary work. You will have to do the hard work of discerning what is right for you given the realities of the culture and society in which you live and the body in which you were born. There are many people who are more threatened in the United States as well as other parts of the world, such as Black, indigenous, and other people of color; transgender people, and gay, lesbian, and queer folks; and people with disabilities. If you're one of these folks, you already know that you need to be more concerned for your physical safety than people who are white, heterosexual, and able-bodied. The threats to your bodily safety in this society are real.

Although I offer tools for increasing your felt sense of safety in this chapter, you will not and should not convince your body that you are safe when you are not. I trust your body. Honor your body's wisdom, especially if it is genetically connected to generations of folks who have endured centuries of violence. Protecting yourself is often necessary, and it would be idealistic and disrespectful for me to suggest that you should think you are safe in public spaces when on many occasions you are not. I want your boundaries to work for you in the reality in which you actually live.

An invitation to explore: In your journal, explore your personal history to discover what you learned about your body and your physical safety.

- How do you feel toward your body?

- How did your mother, father, and any siblings relate to touch and physical boundaries? How did they offer touch or respond to touch?

- What did your family teach you about your right to physical safety?

- How have you taken in any messages from the larger culture about your right to say what is and is not okay for you, physically?

- Is there a way that you would like to adjust your physical boundaries? If so, describe it.

Offer compassion to whatever comes up for you. Use your compassion gesture or give yourself a hug if that feels good to you.

Physical Boundary Practices

The practices that follow will help you get to know your physical boundary comfort zones and increase your brain stem's awareness of relative safety. It is most helpful to work with these boundary practices in a relatively safe environment and away from distractions. I recommend adding just one practice at a time and practicing it for three or four weeks, maybe once a day, maybe less if it brings up a lot. When you are ready, you can then add another practice. Slowly, you will create a state that knows how to experience your physical boundary and your body's safety.

PRACTICE: Color Boundary Outline

This exercise is done using imagery to bring awareness to the sensation of your edges. First, find a comfortable position and notice the space around you. You can stand, sit, or lie down as you do this. Let your eyes slowly notice the space where you are so that you can see that your physical body is not under threat. Take in that in this moment your physical body is relatively safe. Next, close your eyes. Ask yourself, *What color is loving protection?* Let a color come into your mind. Now, let light in that color wash over your body slowly; you might start from the crown of your head and move down over your face and scalp, behind your ears, around the back of your neck. Let the colored light outline every edge of you until the color creates a pool all around your feet. Notice if the color has a hard time reaching any particular parts of your body. Once your whole body is surrounded by the light in your mind's eye, notice how your body is doing. How is your breath responding and what thoughts and feelings do you notice?

Make notes in your journal about your experience. Try this exercise on different days, and notice if the color changes over time or stays the same.

PRACTICE: You've Got Your Back

This is a boundary outline specific to your back. If you have a large startle response or notice that things "come out of nowhere" or tend to feel blindsided by events, this exercise can be helpful. You can do this practice either standing against a wall or seated against the flat headboard of a bed or in a sturdy chair with a solid back. This example uses a wall.

Place your back against the wall so that you can press it firmly into the wall. Now focus your attention where the wall makes contact with your back and notice how it feels: *My back is okay; nothing is coming at my back or hurting my back right now.* Next, roll your back against the wall from side to side. Rock your body so that the wall is in firm contact with different parts of your back—moving side to side or up and down or diagonally. Let your mind follow the firmness of the contact. Do this for a few minutes. How do you feel?

Make notes in your journal about your experience. If you do this practice over time, what shifts happen in how you experience the world? Notice if there are shifts in how you talk to yourself about what you are expecting to happen to you or in how scared or relatively safe you feel from day to day.

PRACTICE: Making Space for You

This exercise is done by pushing things away from your body. It is a good way to feel your power and your right to protect yourself.

Lie down in the middle of a bed or on the floor and surround your body on all sides with heavy pillows. Make sure the pillows feel like they are too close. Now take your hands and push the pillows away from your body. Add your legs in too if it feels right for you, pushing all the heavy pillows away from you until you can feel only the air around your edges. Then say to yourself, *It is okay to take up space. It is okay to make space for me. It is okay to protect myself.* Do this as many times as you want to, until you feel finished.

As an alternative, with the help of a friend or partner, you can do this exercise sitting or standing. You face the other person with your palms touching theirs, and then gently push away their hands to make space for yourself.

Make notes in your journal about your experience. How hard or easy is it to believe the words? Notice what feelings come up for you. Notice if sending this message to yourself is different from messages you have received from other people in your life. Notice if saying other words is a better fit for you. If it is a new message for you to embody, how is that for you? What is it like to let yourself know that your needs are okay and that making space for yourself is safe in this moment?

PRACTICE: Finding Your Ideal Closeness or Distance

This exercise is a great way to get to know what your body likes in terms of closeness and distance from others. You will need a bunch of yarn or string. Pick a roomy spot to do this exercise, either indoors or outside.

You can do this exercise either sitting or standing. Place the yarn on the floor around you to make a tight circle. Now notice what it would be like if another person were with you, at the edge of the yarn. Ask your heart and belly how it would feel to you.

Now, enlarge the circle of yarn, so it is much wider. Make the circle so big that you cannot reach out and touch the yarn from the middle of the circle. Sit or stand in the middle of the circle, as you were before, and notice what it would be like if another person were with you with their body right at the edge of the yarn. Ask your heart and belly how that would feel to you.

Now, play with the yarn, physically reshaping the circle to different sizes. Each time, return to the middle of the circle and imagine a person at the edge of the yarn. Can you find a physical distance that feels better to you than others? What physical distance feels best?

Whom you imagine on the edge of the yarn might matter when finding this distance. What feels right to your body with a stranger may differ from what feels right with a partner or your child. Try this exercise while imagining different people in your life. Find the right distance or closeness that you prefer with each of them.

Take some time to journal about what you discovered. Are you surprised by your body's reactions to certain kinds of closeness or distance? How do you imagine your family history might play into what distance feels safe to you? How do you imagine your romantic history might play into what distance feels safe to you?

Your history will play a big role in your physical boundary needs and wants. Let's follow along with Liliana as she discovers the role of physical boundaries and family learning in her life and relationships.

Process with Liliana

Liliana was a thirty-three-year-old woman who was raised by a single mom in a tight-knit Guatemalan community outside of Houston. Weekdays as a child had been full of many hours in front of the TV, alone in an apartment with the doors locked, as her mom worked long hours as a janitor and had multiple jobs to make ends meet. When I asked if she felt cared for by her mom, she said, "Of course! She worked hard to make sure I had enough. My mom is amazing."

Although they had no other relatives in the United States, weekends were spent at "aunts'" and "uncles'" houses in the extended community. Liliana felt loved and cared for in this community, but she sometimes was made fun of for being less affectionate and welcoming of hugs than the other kids were.

Liliana came to therapy because her girlfriend, Enid, had begged her to. She told me Enid was mad because they had little sex life and didn't touch or cuddle anymore. Enid expressed fear that Liliana didn't love her.

"I do, though. I work hard. I pay for the apartment we live in. I make dinner. Everything we have is nice," she said.

"You show love like your mom did," I reflected to her. "She worked hard and provided to show her love for you. Now do you do that for Enid?"

"Exactly. So why isn't that enough? Why isn't she happy?" Liliana asked.

"I am wondering…you described Enid as warm and cuddly from your first date. She touched you a lot, she leaned in, got close.

I am wondering, did you like that? What made you want to be with her?"

"It's because of that," Liliana answered. "I mean, I am not cold. I like physical affection with my girlfriend. I am close physically with people I am really close to. I want to marry Enid. She's amazing. I love her. I have the ring. I just, I want to fix this thing in me…I don't know why I shut down physically."

Next, Liliana and I tried a physical experiment to help her.

"Can you take one hand and lay it on your leg and now open your hand, like you could set something in it, like I could hand you a big rock and you could hold it?" Liliana placed her hand open on her leg, palm up. "Good. If you want to, place your other hand in your open hand, so the open hand makes a cradle for your other hand." Liliana did this, looking a little skeptical.

"Now imagine you are placing your mind in the hand that's doing the holding. Imagine that the hand being held is your mind, and feel the contact from the cradling hand's point of view. Then switch your focus and feel it from the being-held point of view."

Liliana tried it. After a little while, she said, "That's weird. When I felt into the hand that's getting held, I got really sad, like almost crying sad."

"Can you ask the hand that's being held what is making it sad?" I asked.

Liliana had memories come of reaching out to her mom when she was young. Her mom worked so hard all day that she often responded to Liliana reaching out for hugs or cuddles with annoyance. Her mom wanted physical space at the end of a hard workday, which was hard for Liliana.

"She got this annoyed look on her face," Liliana recalled. "Sometimes she would push my hands off of her, not hard, but patting them and saying 'You're okay,' and she would look bothered."

We tracked when things changed in her relationship with Enid. It was just after they moved in together. Enid had gotten a bad flu. She was in bed for over a week and had been so feverish that any touch felt terrible to her, and she rejected Liliana's attempts to comfort her. When she was moving around the apartment during her illness, she would flinch if Liliana reached out to touch her. "I felt like I was such a bother to her, like I was too much," Liliana said.

After she recovered from the flu, Enid returned to a partner who was much more aloof than she had been previously. Liliana told me, "I wasn't trying to give her the cold shoulder. I guess I just went back to being me. And she doesn't like this version of me."

"So early on in the relationship, the cuddling while bingeing TV shows, the lovemaking, that wasn't you?" I asked. I was wondering if, in the beginning of the relationship, she had pushed herself beyond what felt good for her with her physical boundaries.

"No, that was me too," Liliana said. "I could go back to that. But I am worried about seeing that face again, I think. The one that my mom had, that tells me I'm too much, like I'm needy or whatever."

In our sessions together, Liliana discovered that her natural comfort zone was closer to the rigid side of the physical boundary spectrum with most folks and that with closer people, like her girlfriend or her best friend, she liked being more porous, touching more and accepting more touch. She began using her psychological boundary—a window with rain on it—with Enid to stop taking in the annoyance face as a sign that she was too much. She also used her containing boundary work to pause and support her reaching out more and reengaging physically with Enid. As she outlined her body with color, she started to bring more acceptance and love toward her body. As she did all of these things, her own sense of self-worth improved and so did her relationship.

She left therapy just after she and Enid got married. "I found myself and Enid at the same time," Liliana told me, smiling as she shook my hand at our last good-bye.

Liliana learned how to embrace and accept her own needs for touch and was able to support her physical boundary needs more. Her relationship with herself and her relationship with Enid improved when she did.

Repairing Old Boundary Violations

You have the right to say what touch feels okay and not okay with you at any time. However, knowing what feels okay or not okay may be difficult if you have survived trauma. People who have been through hard things in their history might allow lots of touch from others because they might not know what kind of touch is okay and not with them. If you are one of the many who have a history of your physical boundaries being violated, I am so sorry. This was not your fault. It is normal for our bodies to adapt to those experiences. Sometimes we learn to accept touch that does not feel good to us, and other times we reject physical contact. We might have trouble guessing which scenarios are physically safe and which are less safe. Other times we might seek touch that feels both good and harmful simultaneously, and this can leave us full of confusion. These are all normal adaptations, normal ways of responding to harmful experiences.

Whatever your brain stem learned from the various touch experiences you have had, you can shift that learning if it's no longer working for you. The practices you already learned can help repair old physical boundary violations and increase your body's current sense of safety. They will also increase the accuracy of your assessments of whatever environments you are in, assisting your brain stem in learning what is true for you now. Choose one or two exercises that are particularly resonant and do them many times, so your brain can have more experiences of an integrated state. Increasing your sense of how much safety you have and your own sense of protection will improve your sense of self-worth. To treat yourself like you matter (and I am here to tell you that you do) will help you live into the truth about your worth.

It is all too common for people of all genders and ages to be faced with unwanted touch. Know this: if someone has touched you in ways that feel scary, harmful, or gross to you, you are not at fault for that. You cannot provoke such actions; there is nothing you did to make it happen. If you've had an experience like this, your body might have frozen, or you might have felt like you lost your voice. You did not do anything wrong. It is normal for bodies to be involuntarily still to make it through a time of fear or physical threat.

I want you to feel prepared to add protection for yourself when you can. Start by being curious with yourself about what touch and whose touch feels okay and not okay. You can do this by thinking back to various moments in your life when physical touch made you feel warm and comfortable. You can also look at moments when touch has felt uncomfortable. Think about any similarities you notice in the comfortable scenarios, and then notice if there are similarities in the uncomfortable touch scenarios. This can start to give you an outline of what would feel okay and not okay for your body.

Setting Boundaries Around Unwanted Touch

Once you have a general sense of what feels okay and not okay to you, you can use the six steps to prepare for setting a boundary in moments when physical touch is in your *not okay* category. There are two types of scenarios in which you might need to set a boundary with touch: unwanted touch by someone you do not know and unwanted touch by someone you do know. Let's look at them one at a time.

UNWANTED TOUCH FROM A STRANGER

What would be your big why behind not wanting to accept unwanted touch or closeness from a stranger? Maybe your big why is about respect for your body, or safety. Maybe your big why is about putting loving yourself into action. Find your own reason to speak and act on behalf of your body. This is step 1.

Then define your action (step 2). What is okay for you and what is not okay for you? What will you do if the not okay thing happens? You may also need to consider your safety before taking action, and I support you in trusting yourself to speak up when it is helpful and does not increase danger to do so. When speaking to someone you do not know, there needn't be excuses or explanations about your boundary. It can be helpful to simply state what you do not want.

Then, anticipate possible responses. In these scenarios, many people can become defensive or attempt to undermine the boundary through ridicule. Imagine a past scenario in which you would have liked to say, "Don't touch me," and what might have happened then. When you've made a guess or two, you have finished step 3.

Now for step 4: guess how you might react inside to the other person's response. Would you become angry or embarrassed or feel a need to justify the boundary? Would you try to explain yourself or become harsh in a way that feels more reactive than you want to be, or would you stay grounded?

Next, create a soothing plan (step 5). How will you care for yourself in that moment internally, so you can maintain the boundary in a way that you can feel good about? Plan to do some compassionate self-talk and a gesture that reminds you that you are worthy of protection. Often, reminding yourself of your big why is helpful in step 5.

Then comes step 6, stick to your boundaries. Follow through with words and actions, including walking away, if you can. Remember, boundaries are about what you do in response to the unwanted touch. Trying to get the other person to change their behavior might only escalate the situation.

Process with Carol

Carol worked on this skill and reported using it when out with her girlfriends over the weekend. "This guy came over when my friends and I were at the bar," she said. "He had sent drinks over to us, and we had sent them back, but he wouldn't back off. Then he was leaning over, you know, in my space. He wasn't touching me, but it was too much. So I said, 'That's too close. We're not into this, and we'll have to leave the bar if you can't stop.'

"Then he said, 'I'm just being friendly. What's your deal?' And I put my hand on my belly, like I had practiced, and I told him, 'I said we do not want you to be this close. What you are doing is not okay.' He rolled his eyes at me and left. Before, I would have smiled and dealt with it and tried to make a joke. I thought maybe I was being rude, but actually it felt great. No excuses: if this doesn't feel good to me, I'm saying no."

Often, we are socialized to be more polite and contained than we need to be to protect ourselves and our well-being. Carol made it clear that this stranger's closeness was not okay with her. She did not try to take care of him, or get him to feel good about it, but concentrated instead on what she needed for her safety. She let him walk away and think and feel whatever he needed to while she took care of her own well-being.

UNWANTED TOUCH FROM SOMEONE YOU KNOW

Setting boundaries with people we are close to is often harder than with strangers. Remember, you get to define what is okay touch and what is not okay with you. Let's look at how to use the six steps with someone you know.

Process with Brandon

Brandon had felt uncomfortable with the way his wife touched him when being playful. Often, she would pinch or hit him. He had tried talking to her about it in the past, but so far, she had laughed it off, and any changes she'd made had not lasted. He knew she didn't mean any harm, but it bothered him. He decided he was ready to address it, so he worked out his six steps on paper to prepare for the conversation.

1. Brandon's big why: "I want to feel connected and playful too when she is trying to connect."

2. Defining his action: "I love that we are playful. You are stronger than you think and sometimes get a bit rough with me in a way that doesn't feel good. When that happens, I'll hold your hands and say, 'Careful, Elastigirl,' so we can stay connected and playful but you know I need it to be more gentle."

3. Anticipate her response: "She would laugh and maybe say sorry."

4. Anticipate his own reactions: "I would worry that I hurt her feelings. Then I'd tell her 'Never mind,' to smooth things over."

5. Self-soothing plan: "I will remind myself of my boundary image and that I can trust her. I will use my gesture and say 'connection and honesty' to myself in my head."

6. Say it again and follow through: "I'll say, 'Careful, Elastagirl, don't hurt me,' when I want her to be less rough, and 'I can't help that you picked a sensitive man.'"

You can prepare to make a boundary to protect your body with people you are close to and with people whom you have never met before. If you practice the six steps and use your psychological, containing, and physical boundary work to support you, it will not always be easy, but it will be doable. Knowing where you have fallen in the past on the boundary spectrum and knowing where you'd like to be will support any shifts you'd like to make.

Your Physical Boundary Spectrum

If you spend lots of time on the porous side of the physical boundary spectrum, you might enjoy physical contact and feel like you need lots of it to feel alive and connected. You may have relationships that others might describe as "very touchy." It is also possible that you accept lots of physical contact even if you don't want it. You might touch others too much or too frequently for their comfort and not know it (possibly missing social cues). You might go along with physical or sexual contact that you don't actually want, or you might trust others with your physical well-being even when it's dangerous to do so.

If you are more rigid with your physical boundaries, you might feel uncomfortable with too much touch. You might feel easily overwhelmed by physical touch or feel annoyed when touched by people you don't know well. You might even not like touch at all. You might like space between you and others during conversations and might feel invaded when others lean in, touch you suddenly, or speak very loudly. You might not initiate a lot of physical contact in your gestures or with hugs or touches on arms or shoulders. You might not feel good about frequent sexual contact, or default to not having sex at all. For some folks, this is a natural way of moving through the world that reflects how they feel best in their bodies. For others, there could be difficult or traumatic experiences that have made too much physical closeness feel scary or potentially painful.

Both your genetics and your history play a part in where you fall on this boundary spectrum. Some are born liking more contact and others less. Your history will also play a huge role in your emotional knowings about physical touch. You might have grown up in a landscape without much physical contact, so it might be awkward when people want more touch than feels normal to you. You might also long for more physical closeness, whether that be friendly, romantic, or sexual, but have disgust or fear responses because of hard emotional knowings that come from different forms of trauma and hardship and so move away from contact with others instead of reaching for them.

As with all the boundary categories, healthy expressions of porous and rigid boundaries may also depend on the context. For example, becoming more porous is normal when it comes to cuddling, hugging, and caring for those close to us, like romantic partners, children and family, and friends. Different cultures have different norms with physical touch too; some support lots of contact and others almost none. In work environments, or in situations in which you are in a position of power relative to others, it is normal to be more rigid so that others feel safe. Equally, when you feel your safety and integrity may be compromised, being more rigid can be self-protective.

In our sexual lives, being more porous can deepen intimacy, as long as we are clear that we want the intimate contact at that time and with that person. It's also normal to be more rigid in physical boundaries if you are on the asexual spectrum, have a nervous system that is super touch sensitive, or are very introverted. Each person has the right to determine what physical boundaries they want to hold in different settings and at different times of their lives. Being mindful of our physical needs and effects on others is responsible and relational.

Invitation to explore: Take out your journal and do some writing to discover more about where you currently fall on the physical boundary spectrum.

- *When I focus on my physical boundary…*

- *I go rigid when…*

- *I go porous when…*

Now draw a spectrum line for yourself in your journal, like this:

physical boundary

rigid   porous

First, mark where you are now on this spectrum. Then ask yourself, *Wisest and kindest version of me, where would I like my home base to be?* Then mark that spot.

Moving Forward

In the next chapter, you'll be able to synthesize everything you've learned so far. You will practice the six steps to execute an external boundary with your psychological, containing, and physical boundaries in place to support you. Exciting things happen when you bring it all together.

CHAPTER 6

Using All Your Boundary Skills Together

When I dare to be powerful, to use my strength in the service
of my vision, then it becomes less and less important whether
I am afraid.

—Audre Lorde

It took a long time to learn one set of rules about how to be in relationships
and take care of yourself. Now you've asked your brain to learn a whole new
set of rules and moves. This is hard work and doesn't happen all at once. I
want to celebrate your steps along the way.

Learning New Moves

You are moving in the right direction if you notice any of these signs of
progress:

- In the heat of the moment, you note that you wish to pause and remember your value words and gesture, which is significant even if you don't achieve this.

- You notice that you paused briefly, an important step even if you then fell back into old behaviors. It's still a win, because you used the skill and started building that pathway in your brain.

- After taking someone else's opinion personally, you remember that you could have used your boundary image to keep it outside of you. Remembering this makes it more likely that you will use the image in the future.

- You had a moment of self-compassion.

- You notice that during a conversation, you would have liked to have said, "No, that's not okay with me, and here's what I will do if that happens."

- After something happens, you realize it might be helpful to write in your journal and apply the six steps to a situation like that.

- You know you want to feel more physically safe and have started the practice of outlining your edges with color, and you're sticking with the practice even though not much has changed yet.

These are all important steps. You will likely go through most of them on your way to feeling solid in your boundaries. Celebrate these wins instead of being critical of yourself, because bringing it all together is a process that takes patience. Write down three recent wins in your journal. Changing neural pathways takes time. Every little step matters!

Now let's look at bringing it all together: enacting an external boundary with the help of your psychological, containing, and physical boundaries.

PRACTICE: Bring Your Internal and External Boundaries Together

You will probably want to bring out your journal for this practice so that you can make notes and explore as you go. Bring to mind a difficult situation that you would like to set a boundary around with another person. Slow yourself down so that you can get clear on steps 1 and 2: finding your big why and defining your action.

- In this situation, what is okay for you?

- In this situation, what is not okay for you?

- What's your big why? Define what is so important about addressing the situation.

- What will you do if the not okay thing happens again?

- Write down what you will say to communicate this boundary. (You can follow this guide: "Here's what is okay for me. Here's what is not okay for me. Here is what I will do if or when the not okay thing happens.")

Now imagine you are going to say the words out loud to the person, but don't speak them yet.

Imagine the person as if they were sitting across from you. With them in view, take a moment to outline your edges: imagine a colored light all around your body. Do this to remind your brain stem in its language that your body is safe right now.

Next, let the image of your psychological boundary arise. Make sure to place it between you and the other person. Envision it so that you can look through the image and see the person through the boundary. This reminds you of discernment: you will only take in what is true and about you. It also reminds you of listening with acceptance: you do not need to manage or control the other person's thoughts and feelings, because that person is in the process of becoming themself through time.

Imagine that you take step 2, defining your action by stating the words to the other person. Anticipate their response (step 3). What do they say, do, or express? (Remember that people often have painful emotional experiences in response to boundaries set by others. These feelings are not your fault or anything you need to fix. They are important for that person's resilience and processing of the world; everyone needs their feelings to process what change means for them.)

Let the image of your psychological boundary remain between the two of you so that you do not need to interrupt their feelings, as they make sense of the new messages from you. What do you notice as you keep your psychological boundary up and don't try to change or adjust the other person's feelings?

From this space, anticipate your reaction to their response (step 4). What do you notice about your own feelings and thoughts? Does the other person's response affect you differently when you have inner boundaries in place? Slow down as much as you need so that your psychological boundary image can do its work.

Now add your pause and self-soothing plan (step 5). Breathe. Bring in your containing boundary tools: you can try your compassion gesture and values key words, or it might be that this time something else serves even better. Make the gesture with your body and notice how it feels. Hold the values key words in your mind. Remind yourself why it is important for you to speak your truth about this, why sharing this truth is worthwhile to you.

Think about restating and following through with your boundary in a way that aligns with your relational and personal values and your big why (step 6). After taking a pause between feeling and doing, how would you restate and follow through on your boundary? What happens inside when you imagine sticking to your boundary now?

Well done! Practice makes progress. The more you practice the inner boundary work and the six steps, the more self-trust you will gain and the more confidence you will have in your boundary setting with other people.

Process with Yu-Jin

Yu-Jin wanted to work on an issue that had come up in her family. She was living in Austin, Texas, after moving from the San Francisco Bay Area, where she had grown up and where her family still lived. In Austin, she worked as a graphic designer, and after her father passed away, she began sending money back home every month to help support her mom. She loved that she was able to do this, and she felt very close with her family despite the miles between them.

On a recent visit home, she discovered that her older brother was managing the funds she sent differently than she had expected. Her mother no longer felt that she could afford going to the Korean bathhouse or getting her hair done. She'd always loved to go shopping, but now she wasn't leaving the house, and she seemed depressed. Yu-Jin respected her brother and did not want to challenge him, but she was also concerned for her mom's comfort, which had taken a definite downturn.

Yu-Jin talked with her brother about the changes she saw, and he let her know that he'd shifted how much their mom was able to spend monthly, so they could save more for her long-term care. He was putting most of the money Yu-Jin sent into an investment account instead of leaving it in their mom's checking account. Yu-Jin agreed that future long-term care was important but didn't want her mom's daily comfort to suffer.

Yu-Jin decided to take on a few freelance clients, so she could send home several hundred dollars more each month. She was worried, however, that the increased funds still wouldn't make it to her mom, because her brother might decide to move even more money to the long-term care fund. She knew she would make a request first, but she feared her brother would ignore her wishes.

She used the six steps to help her prepare for a conversation with her brother about how she wanted the funds to be allocated. These were her six steps:

1. Yu-Jin's big why: "I believe my brother is wise to save for the future. Also, my mother's daily comfort and wellness is important to me. I want to take care of her, and I want her to be happy and feel that we honor her."

2. Defining her action: "I will send extra money each month, and I want it to go straight to Mom for her daily expenses now. I want us to work together as a family, so I will send it to the bank account as usual. However, if you see other needs for that money and want to move it out of her bank account, I want to know, so please tell me. I will do my best to help us get what is needed. If you decide to keep moving the money without checking with me first, I will send the money directly to Mom as a check she can cash, and not to the bank account. As long as she is able to manage her own money, I want her to have access to it."

3. Anticipate his response: "He will be quiet, maybe saying, 'That's fine. I will leave the money alone.' I'm guessing he'll be angry or maybe feel ashamed but not say so. He probably won't say much at all, just shut down. If he does show his feelings, it will probably be about the fact that I am not there to help with daily life and I live far away now."

4. Anticipate her own reaction: "Worry and wanting to say 'Never mind' to him."

5. Self-soothing plan: "To move my hands down to my lap and remember my pine tree, then breathe out slowly while remembering the words 'family' and 'care.'"

6. Say it again and follow through: "I will tell him he is doing a great job of caring for Mom; I see that. I will thank him. I am far away and want to pamper her more because I cannot be with her every day. I will say I hope he understands that this is about me and what I want to do for Mom, not because there is anything wrong with how he is doing things. I want the extra money to be used to make Mom happy on a daily basis, while we also save for her long-term care."

Yu-Jin's work on psychological boundaries and containing boundaries intertwined in our work together. Her initial boundary image was a beautiful river, which represented not taking in what wasn't about her and didn't feel true to her. As she practiced with this image, she realized the river wasn't helping her enough to accept others' feelings. She had always tried to smooth over hard feelings, and it was a new idea that someone's unpleasant feeling, such as sadness or anger, might be helpful to them. When she looked at her own experiences of sadness, anger, and shame, she found that such moments held clarity and growth for her, even though they were painful. As she held this idea, her psychological boundary image transformed into a pine tree. For Yu-Jin, the pine tree represented deep wisdom and groundedness. When she put the pine tree between herself and another person, it helped her feel like she was allowed to have her boundaries and didn't need to make the other person feel better in the moment.

Yu-Jin was concerned about how her behavior affected others, and so her relational integrity values were rooted in being slow, thoughtful, and gentle. Her big growth in her containing boundary work was risking sharing her truth more often, even when difficult feelings might come up. Her gesture of putting her hands in her lap, open, was a reminder to open her heart when it felt right for her to do this. Opening up and sharing more is always vulnerable. Breathing through this and having her pine tree image helped her feel more protected. When she felt more protected, she stayed more integrated while she risked sharing her heart.

Boundaries and Family of Origin

Yu-Jin lived hundreds of miles away from her family and planned to do her boundary setting over Facetime. If she were in person with her family, she might have needed to spend more time preparing and self-soothing, and it may have been harder to stick with the six steps, the internal boundary work, and treating herself well.

Your family of origin can be one of the most challenging spaces to use these boundary setting tools. There are a few good reasons for this. Your brain is always using environmental cues to guess which parts of your psychological floor will be most relevant to the current moment. When you are around the family you grew up with, your brain will get old cues from smells, faces, tones of voice, and patterns of interactions. If you are visiting the place you grew up, all the light, sounds and smells, and energies from there will also cue your brain to use older maps. This means that your old ways of feeling, reacting, and doing boundaries will be primed and ready. It will be more challenging to use your new tools, and you may revert to old responses you thought you had outgrown. This is normal. Don't despair. Slow down, love yourself, and try again.

Since it is easier to use these tools in newer relationships and environments than with your family of origin, do not use a home visit as your only gauge of success or failure. When you are first working on new boundaries, it's good to practice many boundary interactions with yourself and others in the here and now before you try to level up and use your skills with your family of origin—during the holidays, for example. Be gentle with yourself and make sure to build in lots of opportunities to pause. Remind yourself of who you are and why you are doing this hard work.

Moving Forward

Sometimes the change we want is not from someone else. It's from ourselves. Let's look at how you can use the six steps in the creation of your own behavior change: setting boundaries with yourself.

CHAPTER 7

Setting Boundaries with Yourself

Life isn't perfect, any failures you have are actually learning moments. They teach us how to grow and evolve.

—Phillipa Soo

I'm happy to share that you can also use the six steps internally to make behavior changes, set boundaries with yourself, and reach your goals. Doing this will help you shape your life with intention and move forward in the ways that you want to grow. In this chapter, we will look at shifting a problematic behavior that you'd like to change, calming an inner critic voice, and announcing a change to others.

Making a Behavior Change

Often, we have behaviors that don't serve us, yet we continue doing them. No matter how many times we try or we resolve to stop doing that thing and start doing this other thing, we find ourselves repeating the familiar behavior. Everyone has something like this, in some form. Believe me, you are not alone. When you want to change a behavior that is habitual or compulsive, you can use the six steps and your boundary work to help you with the shift.

What changes would you like to make for yourself? Maybe you want to stop emotionally eating or shopping, or maybe you tend to drink one too many cocktails when out with friends, or maybe you feel like your screen time is out of control. Maybe you want to talk less and listen more or you want to be more mindful about raising your voice. Maybe you are working on a more serious goal like shifting an addictive behavior or ceasing to do something that's damaging your work life, relationships, or connection with yourself. Regardless of what behavior you wish to change, you can use the six steps and your internal boundaries to make the change doable.

Identify the Behavior

First, identify the behavior you want to change. Once you have identified it, start thinking about what hopes might be behind this behavior. Is this behavior rewarding yourself for something? Is it about getting things to work out the way you want them to? Is it a distraction from some other pain? When you can understand what needs are being served by the behavior you want to change, you can start getting creative about other, less costly ways to meet these needs. So, take some time to really think about the hopes or wishes behind the behavior.

An invitation to explore: Explore a behavior you'd like to change.

- What behavior would you like to change?

- When did this behavior start?

- When does this behavior happen? See if you discern a pattern or if it is more random.

- Ask yourself, *What needs get met when I do this? How does it serve me?*

- Ask, *What is the cost to me of doing this? How does it disserve me?*

- Does the behavior reflect your sense of integrity? Does it align with who you want to be?

- Are there other ways the need can be met? What are they?

- What are you willing to try?

Now that you have explored the behavior that you want to focus on, you can use the six steps and your containing boundary work to make a shift. First, you will need to find your big why. The bigger the behavior, habit, or compulsion, the bigger your why is going to need to be, so really dig in.

Let's look at Diego's process. Diego is a dad who wanted to address his habit of emotional eating and to develop a healthier relationship with food.

Process with Diego

"Food meant love growing up. Now, when I feel lonely, I eat. When I feel sad, I eat. When I want a reward, I eat. I think for me it's about love, like showing love to myself. I give my kids ice cream or cake when I want them to know I love them. But it's hurting my health now. I want to change this. I don't want food to mean love anymore," he said.

Diego's issue was big, so his *why* needed to be big too.

"I really love my kids and my wife. I want to be around for them. If I don't stop this, I'll get diabetes like my dad. He didn't take care of himself, and he died so young. He was just fifty-six years old," Diego recalled. "I need to stop it, because I don't want to leave them. I don't want them to have to miss me when they are in high school like I had to with my dad."

Diego defined his action after he found his big why, using the boundary map of "Here's what is okay with me, here's what's not okay with me, and here's what I will do when the not okay thing happens."

"I love showing love, and there are lots of ways to do that. Showing love through sweets and sugar isn't okay with me anymore. I know it's not good for my kids in the long run. When I want to show love to myself or to my kids or to my wife, I will stop myself with my containing boundary—putting my hands together and thinking the words 'community' and 'big heart'—and then show my love through playing with my kids or hugging my wife. I'll tell myself I am doing a hard thing to be a good dad. In that moment, I will not eat sweets or feed my kids sweets. I'll play games with them instead."

What's your big why? Make sure it is big enough to give you the emotional juice you will need to follow through.

An invitation to explore: Use these prompts to find your big why and define your action.

- *The reason I want to make a change with this behavior is…*

- *What is okay with me?*

- *What is not okay with me?*

- *What will I do to stop the behavior? How will I redirect myself to get the need met in a different way?*

Once you define your action, anticipate your internal responses in the moment when the behavior is likely to happen. How will you feel? What will happen inside you? Remember you can always use your containing boundary here to add a pause between feelings and behavior.

It is normal to have hard emotions come up when you set a boundary with yourself. Working through steps 3, 4, and 5 will help you stick to your boundary in step 6. I want you to be able to anticipate if there are feelings and longings in you that do not like this new boundary.

Make a Self-Soothing Plan

A self-soothing plan can help you stick to your boundary. This plan can involve doing something else that feels good and soothes you but is not connected to the behavior you're trying to change. Stick to your boundary without internal harshness, and comfort yourself when needed.

I asked Diego about what might happen inside him when he wanted to eat or feed his kids sweets but stopped himself.

"I'll get so mad," he told me. "I like what I like. I don't want to have limits like this."

"When you get mad, what will happen next? Will you just stay circling in mad, or will something else happen inside?" I asked him.

"I usually say, 'Better to be eating than be mad.' Then I flex and break my rules with myself, and I break down and eat a lot. Then I feel guilty, and then I eat more to give myself some love even though I feel bad. It's a whole cycle," he answered.

"Great awareness," I told him. "What happens if you use your gesture and your words to soothe the mad feeling?" I asked him.

"Oh, like my pause gesture?" He put his hands together. "That would work, I think, and also I need to do something loving toward myself, like tell myself I am making good dad choices. Then I'll feel better."

Having internal contradictions and conflict is normal, because there are many neural networks in your brain, and not all of them have the same knowings. It's easy to see how these neural networks are parts of yourself. You can watch your mind and see, for example, one part of you really wants the sweets and another part of you doesn't want the consequences of eating sweets too often. This is completely normal. If you resist the behavior changes you decide on, it doesn't mean you are failing or are bad at boundaries with yourself. It means your brain is currently still processing what this change might mean to you across many different neural networks with different maps about how to take care of yourself. Your brain is tracking whether or not your needs are still going to be met if you change the behavior. Your brain works to get your needs met the best it can, even if its current methods have a high cost.

As you set your boundary and keep it, you will build trust in yourself, and your brain will experience that there are indeed multiple ways to meet the same need.

An invitation to explore: Use this journal exercise to anticipate possible internal responses to your boundary and develop a soothing plan.

- Imagine yourself in a situation when the behavior that you want to change normally happens. Let yourself into that moment: imagine the room, the air, the time of day. Imagine your body is about to do the behavior. Write down the feelings and body movements that might happen right before the behavior starts.

- Imagine you follow through on your action (step 2). Great job, boundary setter! What are you feeling? How are you talking to yourself? (step 3)

- What happens next? Do you want to go back to the old behavior? Do you speak to yourself harshly or try to force yourself into compliance? Or do you speak gently to yourself and say compassionate things? (step 4)

- Make your self-soothing plan. What are you going to do to treat yourself with both kindness and firmness when you feel resistance to doing something different? (step 5)

- Stick to your new plan in your mind's eye. What do you feel toward yourself when you see yourself doing what you promised you would do? (step 6)

Can you commit to this change for yourself? When you try out your boundary in real life, you might discover that tweaks need to be made to your soothing plan. Come back to these steps again and again as you find what's right for you.

Think of this work as a practice to do again and again, slowly learning to trust yourself over time. You do not need to be perfect to trust yourself; instead, trust yourself to keep trying. Slipping up is normal and common; we all slip up at times when we endeavor to change our own behavior. The brain builds different connections and new pathways slowly, but it builds them surely and more solidly if done with love (Neff 2011). If making a change feels as awkward as learning to ride a unicycle, then you are probably doing it right.

Next, I want to look at how you can use these steps to shift how you talk to yourself. If you have a voice in your head that's not kind to you, that's the voice of the inner critic. You can shift everything by setting a boundary with this harsh voice in your head.

Making a Boundary with Your Inner Critic

Most of us have voices inside ourselves that can say mean things to us. Doing psychological boundary work and the six steps internally can help shift your relationship with this inner critic.

Process with Sharon

Sharon had a harsh inner voice that called her terrible names. Sharon worked on this boundary practice by finding a twisting in her belly that always went with the inner voice.

"Put your boundary image between who you are and that twist in your belly," I said.

"The boundary image where I push from my heart out, like I am pushing someone away to create more space?" Sharon asked.

"Yes, put that push-away gesture between you and the twist in your belly, in your mind's eye. That gesture knows discernment, so it won't let you take in anything that is not about you and not true. And that gesture also knows listening with acceptance—it knows that this part of you in your belly is doing the best it can and becoming itself through time, so we don't have to change the feeling in your belly."

"Okay," Sharon said, her eyes closed, hands pushing. "When I put my image up, it calms down. The voice in my head changes from an angry tone to more like...pleading?" Sharon tracked. "My belly and that twisting feeling say, 'You never do anything right. You're a loser and a faker.' But that's not true. When I hear it through the boundary, I know that's not true. I don't have to believe it. I wonder what it wants for me?"

As her brain had more protection and stayed more integrated, Sharon's natural curiosity rose up. She discovered that the inner critic was trying to protect her from some future shame or failure by keeping her small.

What might you discover about your inner critic voice if you let yourself connect to it with inner protection in place? This first thing to do is to find your inner critic voice. What does it sound like? It might have a sensation in your body or words that go with it, or you might have an image of who this voice belongs to, within you. Imagine that the inner critic has a body and face. How does it look? What would it be called, if it had a name? Try this journal work to add in the protection of the psychological boundary before you work through your six steps.

An invitation to explore: Recall a moment when your inner critic voice was working overtime. Let yourself sink into that moment in your memory, so you can track the voice and find it within. Use these prompts:

- When you notice the voice, where do you feel it in your body?

- What does the voice often say?

- When you notice that voice, what image comes to mind?

- Now say to yourself, *This voice is not all of me, not all of who I am.* Place your boundary image or gesture between you and that sensation, voice, or image.

- What do you notice now? How do you feel toward that voice?

- Feel free to ask the voice any questions you have about its hopes for you or fears for you. Ask how it learned to use criticism to help you.

- Thank the voice for trying to help you in the past.

Now that you have a bit more brain integration while you are in relationship with this part of you, try using your six steps to create a kind and firm boundary with your inner critic.

Start with your big why. What is so important about changing your relationship with your inner critic? How does your inner critic get in your way? What could you accomplish or do if that negative voice was not so loud? Having a loud inner critic is costly and painful, for sure. Research shows that behavioral change and courage are noted to be much higher and longer lasting in those who use self-compassion than those who use self-criticism to make shifts (Neff 2011).

Next, define your action: decide what you are going to do when the inner critic gets going. Keep in mind this is not about changing the voice of the inner critic. It is about shifting what *you* do when a thing that is not okay happens. When you hear the voice, you might decide that you'll stop everything you're doing to make sure your psychological boundary image is in place, so you don't take in untrue words. Or you might decide to put on music, so you can hear other things besides the inner critic. Or you might decide to talk directly to your inner critic, like this: *The way you are speaking to me is not okay with me. I will stop making decisions and moving forward while you do that.* You might even do something playful, like break into a goofy dance every time you hear the voice get going with words or critiques that are not okay.

Try addressing the inner critic as "you" and speaking directly to it as if it were a person sitting beside you or inside you. This might sound like, *I want to do things really well too, and pushing myself to strive is okay with me. The way you talk to me is not. From now on, when I hear you talk to me like that or tell me those untrue things, I will put on music and dance instead of believing you.* Speaking to the voice this way resonates with the reality that this voice and way of thinking is only one complex neural network in you and not all of you.

Be creative as you define what is okay for you, what is not okay for you, and what you will do when the not okay thing happens. After you make your plan, move on to step 3 to anticipate what the voice might do. Will it get louder and harsher, go silent, move to sadness? Will it become more insistent, or will it die down?

Then do step 4. How will you react next? Will you have feelings that will make your plan harder to stick to?

Once you know this inner landscape, make a self-soothing plan. Maybe you can send some kindness to your inner critic, too. I hug mine and thank her for trying to make sure I do well. I let her know I care about that too, even when I'm asking her to speak differently. As you think through your steps, solidify your thoughts with this journaling work.

An invitation to explore: Write down the six steps you will use when your inner critic gets going. Place your boundary image in between you and your inner critic as you write. Use these prompts:

- *Having a boundary with my inner critic is important to me because…*

- *Here's what is okay with me and what is not okay with me…*

- *Here's what I will do when the not okay thing happens…*

- *When I do this, it is likely that my inner critic will…*

- *When that happens, I will likely feel and think…*

- *My plan for soothing those thoughts and feelings is…*

- *Here's how I will stick to my new boundary…*

Good work using this process to transform harsh ways you might speak to yourself! Next, let's look at the six steps to let others know about a change you are making.

Using the Six Steps to Support a Change

Things often change in life, and our assessments of what we need change over time, too. Sometimes you will need to set a boundary with others because of a change you have made internally, and you need to communicate it. Perhaps your work-life balance is off, or maybe you enjoy being with a certain friend but not every night of the week. Perhaps you have been in a partnership without voicing discontent, and the time has come to say more. When these circumstances arise, it can often be helpful to let others know about the change we are making. You can use the six steps to help you communicate about a change.

First, find your big why. What is important about making this change? Why is it worth it to change this? Is it kinder to let others know about the shift in a clear way than to make the change indirectly, unclearly, or in secret?

Let's look at Marion's journey.

Process with Marion

Marion was a landscape architect and business owner. She needed to make a shift in her business practices. She invoiced her clients regularly but would continue doing their work on time even if the payments were late. It had become a problem that was threatening her stability and home. "I am afraid they will all fire me if I change this, but I have to. I was two weeks late on my mortgage this month."

Marion decided to let her clients know that she would be pausing her work on their projects until their accounts were up to date. "I want to explain how behind I am in paying bills," she said. "That way they'll understand why I desperately need this." I asked her to use her containing boundaries to pause and wonder about what information she wanted to pass on and what information she didn't want to share. As she paused, she discovered she was trying to keep her clients from being mad at her, and that they didn't need information about her personal finances.

When setting a boundary, many people tend to overexplain and manage the feelings of others to try to mitigate any backlash. I asked Marion to use her boundary image and her pause to help herself find the words for step 2, defining your action. I reminded her that it's helpful to start by acknowledging that a change is happening.

Marion landed on, "I am making a change in my billing policy. Going forward, I will not continue the next phase of the project until invoices are paid in full for the phase that has been completed."

Do you want to make a change? Would it be kind to let others who are affected by it know that? You can use your journal to work through your six steps to practice sharing a change without overly managing the feelings and reactions of others.

You might find that as you start to bring your voice into the world, people will surprise you. They may be calmer and more accepting than you anticipate. If that happens, let yourself be pleasantly surprised. Your history may make you expect people to have a certain kind of reaction, but if you can notice that something unexpected is happening, it can make permanent shifts to what your subcortical brain expects in the future.

People may also not surprise you. Pushback is common. When Marion set her new boundary, many of her clients understood and paid up immediately. Two of her clients did not react calmly to the change, and she used her containing boundary to uphold her decision to stop work until she was paid. One of those two clients responded to her calm firmness by paying her, and the other pushed back several times and then left, disgruntled.

When Boundaries Lead to a Rupture

Sometimes when you set a boundary, people will not respect it, and this can lead to a rupture. This is a hard reality. Sometimes the rupture can be repaired, and other times not. Letting go of managing the outcome and the behavior and feelings of others means taking more responsibility for protecting yourself and treating yourself as a person worthy of protection and kindness.

When Marion set her boundary, she was afraid that all her clients would leave her, but she knew she was treating herself poorly by doing work without timely compensation. She was not demanding that her clients pay her; instead, she was honoring their original agreement, which she had been breaking. The agreement was that she would do certain work, and her clients would pay for it. Doing work without pay was not the agreement.

When she shifted her behavior to match the agreement—no more work without pay—the clients generally honored the original agreement and paid. To do this peacefully within herself, she had to let go of the idea of *getting them to pay her* and instead tell herself, *I do work when paid on time. I do not continue working without pay.*

At the same time that you let go of managing the behaviors and feelings of others, you can be curious about what is happening inside *them* if you get a lot of pushback and boundary testing.

Boundary testing is normal. It is not fun to receive, but it is common. Can you think of a time when someone set a boundary with you? Did you accept it calmly? Did you feel hurt or agitated? Did you try to negotiate or talk them out of their boundary? We are all trying to get our needs and wants met. It is common to try to get around what we experience as roadblocks.

Sticking to your boundary in the face of boundary testing will build your self-trust. If you think about it as, *There's a person trying to get what they want*, rather than *They are disrespecting me*, it can help you feel less agitated when others try to negotiate, go around your boundary, or push back.

Thinking about boundary testing with curiosity rather than judgment often helps to keep your brain integrated. When your brain goes into judgment, you are more likely to lose your containing boundary and less likely to pause between what you feel and what you do. This could lead to acting in ways that you later regret. I want you to be firm with your boundaries and to hold to your choice when pushback comes. This firm stance will be more peaceful and more flexible if your brain is in a more integrated state.

The other good news in thinking about it as *This is a person trying to get what they want* is that it helps you to live in real equality with others. This is a sharing-power position. This is not about who gets their way. It is not about bullying anyone or manipulating people to show up for you the way you want them to. Instead, this way of thinking is based in trust. You trust them to navigate disappointment or hurt or anger when they try and fail to get things to go their way, and you trust yourself to make choices that align with your well-being.

Moving Forward

In addition to using the six steps to create behavioral change, to protect yourself from harsh inner voices, and to announce a change, you can also use the process to move into deeper connection with others and be more vulnerable with people you want to be close to and emotionally intimate with. The next chapter will look at increasing openness in close relationships.

CHAPTER 8

Boundaries and Openness in Close Relationships

Love is a combination of…care, commitment, knowledge, responsibility, respect, and trust.

—bell hooks

Naming your requests and boundaries is vulnerable. Ultimately, it is an act of love that you do to strengthen and protect a relationship. It lets other people know you better, so it's a gift. It may involve temporarily rough waters, but it gives both people a sturdier boat and a more reliable compass for their journey together. Being clear with your boundaries (both the internal and the external ones) lets you be more open and present with the people that you long for closeness and intimacy with.

For those who tend to share less and rarely risk rocking the boat, there is often no pause between having hard feelings or longings and a move to pull away, hide, or be silent. Avoiding your partner's response or the risk of rejection can lead to not being known. This chapter will show you how to use internal boundaries and the six steps to become more vulnerable with others and risk being more fully seen.

Using Your Boundaries to Open Up

It is normal, when worrying about being hurt or concerned about angering or hurting someone we care about, to avoid risky endeavors like speaking the truth, but we can't feel connected unless we are open with the people around us (Brown 2011). To get there, you will need to put a pause between the feeling of fear and whatever withdrawal or concealment moves you might be inclined to do.

The first thing you'll need is a big why that is big enough to make it worth facing your fear head-on. Do you want more intimacy or want to be known better? Perhaps you are hoping that you can get more of what you want and need. Perhaps loneliness is too present, and you want to deepen the connections you have or find new connections where you can be authentic. Whatever your reason, it is probably linked to your values, which you explored in the containing boundaries work you have done (see chapter 4). Find a reason and let the hope behind that reason fill you up. Is the hope big enough that it will be worth facing the fear and stress that comes from speaking up?

You will also want to make sure to use your psychological boundary image. This will help you be curious about whatever response you receive to increased sharing, rather than become defensive or shut down automatically if your partner's response is not what you hoped for.

Process with Leo

"I do want Will to know me better, and I want to get more of what I want. I always do what he wants. If he asks where we should eat, I say, 'I'm easy; you choose.' When it comes to how we spend free time, I say, 'Whatever you want is great.' I worry so much about a disagreement, I just don't speak up. But that goes against my values: authenticity and connection," Leo said. Then he paused, thinking.

"I've got it," he said. "I am making a change and saying more, but the real shift is inside. What I say to myself is, 'It is okay to be known, it is not okay to not be known, so I am going to tell him more of what I want and like.' Oooh, that makes me shaky inside. I'll say, 'Will, I don't push myself enough to tell you what I want. That's not on you, that's on me. I want to say more. When you ask me where we might go to dinner, I'll tell you what I want next time. If you don't want the same thing, that's okay, and we'll work it out.'" Leo let out a big breath.

"And remember your waterfall image," I reminded him.

"Good, yeah, the waterfall helps...it's still freaky, but I can do it," Leo said.

Once you find the words for what you want to share with someone else, then take some guesses about how you will feel when you share more of yourself. Will you be shaky like Leo? Will you be harsh with yourself, saying you are not worth it? Would you move into despair, like, *Speaking up never did me any good?* Or would you feel exhilarated to be taking the risk of sharing the real you? You might need to treat speaking up as an internal behavior change and do the six steps with yourself. Your containing boundary work will support you in pausing before choosing silence; inside the pause, you can support yourself in opening up.

Remember your psychological boundary, so you protect your mind and heart from unnecessary hurt and protect your partner's mind from you too. If the answer you get back when you share more is what you had hoped for, having your image up will help you be present in that moment. If the answer you get back when you share more is not what you had hoped for, your psychological boundary image can help you discern if the reaction that comes your way is really about you and true or if it is information about this person whom you love and are trying to be closer to. Your boundary image will help you witness their feelings and thoughts without having to change them for you to be okay. Having this inner boundary in place also helps you risk vulnerability again, because it builds trust in yourself. You grow to know that you will be okay, whether the reaction from the other person is ideal or not.

You can use these tools to share everyday things like Leo did and also support yourself in more risky shares, so you can be in more integrated brain states as you move into courage and vulnerability.

An invitation to explore: Use this inner work to increase your vulnerability and share more of yourself with others. Ask yourself:

- *What is one thing that I would like to share with someone I am close with but I hold back from sharing?*

- *What is the cost of not speaking, not being vulnerable?*

- *What good might come if I shared more of myself?*

- *When I think of sharing this with my boundary image in between us, I notice…*

- *I plan to make the next vulnerable connection by saying or doing…*

You now have a plan to share more of yourself with someone you care about. You can use your containing boundary pause to slow down and hold yourself in compassion and in your values as you say the things that are hard for you to say.

Remember that you can be discerning about whom you choose to share more with. Not everyone you run into will be trustworthy. If you are with someone who is not available to support vulnerable and close connection, you can use your containing boundary to choose to share less. With people who want to show up and support you, you can use your pause to support yourself in moving along the boundary spectrum to a more porous position than you sometimes take. Your psychological boundary will support you in staying more protected as you open up, because even trustworthy people will not be there in all the ways you hope every time.

You also can use these same psychological and containing boundaries to become a better listener. When you choose to take on supporting someone close to you in their vulnerability, you can employ your psychological boundary image to help you stay curious about what they are sharing about their experience of the world. How would you like to be held when you share? Does that way feel supportive for them? This space between you allows for curiosity about their processes and needs and allows you to be open to them having different needs than you might have when you are vulnerable.

You can also use your containing boundary in the listener position. When you use your pause and value words, you can keep your answers in alignment with your integrity and relational values as you show up for the other person's bid for connection. Perhaps your containing boundary will help you say less and listen more. Perhaps it will guide you to be gentle or kind or even open to sharing more of yourself in return.

Setting Boundaries with Partners

There are times when something won't be working as well as you would like in a relationship. In times like these you will probably start by making a request. You can be clear about what you are asking for and be open to negotiating potential solutions to whatever dilemma you are facing. Your internal boundaries will support you in being more open to requests from loved ones and in making requests of others in ways that are kind.

At times, your requests won't give you the outcomes you are hoping for. When that happens, it will be important to get clear with yourself about what is and is not okay with you. I notice sometimes folks skip becoming clear with themselves and try to set a boundary without clarity, and this can be a recipe for difficult times. Perhaps after making a request, the way you were hoping things would go has not happened, and it turns out that, though it is not ideal, things are actually okay. Then you will feel the grief or loss of whatever you are not getting and can also celebrate the things you are getting. Other times, you will see that things are not okay. When you do decide that setting a boundary is the right move, you can use the six steps to prepare you for the conversation and your actions.

Process with Val

Val had asked repeatedly for more help with dinner prep and meal planning. Both Val and her partner, Joey, worked full-time, and they had fallen into the habit of Val being the one in charge of meals because she liked to cook more than he did. That was before they had kids. Joey said he would take over more of the planning and cooking, but hadn't. Val worked through her six steps.

1. Val's big why: "I do not want to build resentment, and I need Joey to support me. We have two kids under five, and I need more help. I am exhausted."

2. Defining her action: "It is okay with me to work together. It would be okay with me to plan meals all the time if he took on something else, so I am not so overwhelmed. It is not okay with me to have it automatically fall on me and not talk about it. I want us to make a plan and stick to it. I will tell him we can create a plan together, or I will hire a company to do most of the dinners for us."

3. Anticipate his response: "He will be mad. He will roll his eyes and tell me I am making a big deal out of things."

4. Anticipate her own reactions: "I am defensive. I want to argue with him that it is a big deal." Then Val remembered her psychological boundary image. "Whew. I put up my ring of monster truck tires. Now I feel clear. I am not overreacting. My feelings and overwhelm are real."

5. Self-soothing plan: "I will twist my wedding ring and say in my head 'self-trust' and 'kindness.'"

6. Say it again and follow through: "I will say, 'I get that you are not feeling like I am, but this is true for me. Either we can make a time to sit down and have a conversation about this by the end of the weekend, or I will look into getting the help I need in a different way.' Then I will leave the room and breathe. I will wait to see what he does."

After coming up with her six steps, Val said, "I am just saying, 'Here's how to help. If you can't or don't want to, then I will help me.' I feel stronger and less frustrated."

You can be creative with your actions and boundaries. Your actions will impact the people you are closest to. This will often evoke some sort of change. Perhaps the changes will lead to more closeness and more trust so that you can navigate hard things together. Perhaps it will lead to harder outcomes. You can keep setting boundaries as you need to, so your actions will stay aligned with your integrity and relational values in your intimate and close relationships.

Acknowledging Deal Breakers

I can't tell you what's healthy or unhealthy when it comes to defining your deal breakers in relationships. There are many good and complex reasons to stop yourself from completely walking away. I also want to support you in grieving this fact: if you want to be in a relationship, you will not always get all that you want. Both people have wants and needs, and sometimes they will be in conflict, and negotiation will be needed.

When you think about setting boundaries in your important relationships, be creative in what you might do in response to the thing that is not okay with you. Try it out in your mind before you share it to see if it feels congruent with what you believe and consistent with your integrity. Prior to setting a boundary about ending a relationship, see if you can set other boundaries to shift the emotional landscape for you. You could say something like "Our distance and my loneliness is not okay with me. I will keep bringing up longing to be closer to you and inviting you to talk to me more. If you have a different plan, that would help. I am open to hearing it"; or "There is too much drinking at your office parties for me to be comfortable, so I will not go anymore"; or "I am going to spend the holidays at our house and not at your family's house next year, and I hope you will join me, but I'll understand if you don't."

If you have ascertained that the issue is a true deal breaker for the relationship, it is important to acknowledge that fact. The choice to leave a relationship if a not okay thing happens again is a firm and serious boundary. I trust that you will know when ending a relationship is the right thing to do.

More Protection, More Connection

Sometimes we wish there were an easy solution to make hard or vulnerable conversations feel smooth and pain-free. In my experience, there is no way to do that and be authentic and connected. Paths that feel faster and easier in the moment, like judgment, distancing, avoiding, or managing the other, are costly in the long run.

You can choose the harder-in-the-moment road of vulnerability and courage and can, with practice, feel more protected. The more protected you feel, the more your brain will perceive that things are okay; even that tough conversations are okay. The more that happens, the more you will be able to stay in an integrated brain state with creativity, connection, and less reactivity. Hard conversations can have more authenticity, more respect, and better outcomes.

I also acknowledge the reality that even when you do all you can to speak with kindness and clarity, to increase your protection and receptivity, to share authentically and listen to others deeply, things can still go awry. Things can go wonderfully, and things can go badly. Ruptures are sometimes permanent. For this reason, becoming familiar with your own grief is a beneficial practice.

Moving Forward

The next chapter will look at both the love in action and the grief that are often a part of deep boundary work.

CHAPTER 9

Clear Is Kind

You might as well answer the door, my child,
the truth is furiously knocking.

—Lucille Clifton

When you protect yourself, psychologically, physically, and interpersonally, you are treating yourself like a person worthy of protecting. When you take the time to wonder, *What is okay with me and not okay with me?* you treat yourself as a person who is worthy of being listened to and believed. When you add a pause between what you feel and what you do, and draw on your values, you are treating yourself as someone trustworthy who lives in their integrity. When you hold yourself in deep compassion and another person in equal compassion at the same time, clarity about your boundaries will emerge.

If you know that whatever is happening for the other person is understandable for them (and maybe even coming from old pain or fear), and hold whatever is happening with an awareness of how hard it is to have a pause when we are hurting or scared, then kindness toward them will emerge. Then you hold the other person with deep kindness as another bumbling human trying to get through this life, and you hold on to your own needs equally. When you do this, you will stop trying to get the other person to change. Instead, you will see what you need to do for yourself. Clarity about what boundary would be ideal for you will come. Communicating it clearly is an act of love toward yourself and the other person. Maybe this clear communication will change something; maybe it will not. Either way it goes, you held deep compassion for both of you at once.

Love Toward Self

You are worthy of having a voice. You are worthy of standing up and saying "This thing isn't okay with me, and so here's what I am going to do to take care of myself, even if you don't get it or agree." Sometimes others will not agree or will not even understand why you have an issue. That can make for a hard moment, but you are worthy of being believed. How you see the world does matter. You don't have to get others to see things your way. You don't need to convince them that your boundary is justified. In fact, letting go of a need for them to agree with you before you set your boundary will increase your self-trust.

If you can say, *Others don't get it, but I still believe that, for me, this is how it is,* that's an act of trusting yourself. As you act in ways that are self-trusting, your mind and body will receive that information and risk saying more to you about who you are. The more you act like you believe yourself, the clearer the information you get from your subcortical brain and body.

The more you know about what is and is not okay with you, the more you trust yourself, the more you see yourself clearly, and the more you treat yourself as if you deserve to be listened to and believed, these add up over time, as you are treating yourself like you are worthy of love. What is love? I believe love is an embodied acknowledgment of the reality of worth.

When you pause to live in your integrity, when you listen to and believe your body about what feels safe and not, you put into action your worthiness. When you listen to others' ways of thinking and feeling without losing your own sense of what feels true, you treat them as beings of worth without losing your worth. The more your actions align with what feels okay and not okay with you, the more you treat yourself like you are a being of high worth. This boundary work is self-love in action.

Love Toward Others

Using your containing boundary means you are being thoughtful, not just about your integrity but also about how you affect others and about how your actions lead to more or less closeness, clarity, and kindness. The more you think about the ways you affect others, the more likely you'll treat them respectfully. This work empowers you to trust yourself more while communicating to the other people in your life that they are also worthy of your hard work. This is love in action toward others.

When you have a psychological boundary between you and others, it allows for more connection. This is because you have increased your safety, which helps you listen to them without trying to adjust, change, or control what they are thinking and feeling. As they receive this deep listening from you, they will feel your acceptance, respect, and kindness even through moments of disagreement. To be believed and disagreed with, to be respected and have kindness come toward them even during a disagreement, is a rare gift. It's a deeply loving gift that you can give to those around you every day.

When you risk letting others know what you want through requests instead of complaints or demands, you move toward them with vulnerability. When you can handle a no and negotiate with them to find a way you can both say yes while taking care of yourselves, you show others that you respect them enough to want to know their truth, too. It is an act of vulnerability and love to let another person know what is not okay with you while not trying to manage their feelings. When you do this, you trust them to make sense of the world. You trust them to handle their feelings and thoughts and share with you what feels right. Even in moments of unhappiness, they will often feel the care you give them as you trust them to handle their own feelings, while not leaving them alone. Complaint is a power-under position, demand is a power-over position, and request and boundary-setting are power-with, power-sharing strategies.

In their book, *The Power of Discord*, Ed Tronick and Claudia Gold (2020) note that trust is built in the relationship between any two people not primarily through moments of peace and connection but through moments of disagreement, discord, and struggle—while staying connected and not abandoning each other. Your inner boundary work will support you staying in connection while you risk rocking the boat through your direct requests and six steps, so you can bring more of who you really are to your relationships. As you stick through these hard moments, the people in your life will gain trust in you, gain confidence in the resiliency of your relationship, and receive more respect from you. This adds to the love and resiliency within all of your relationships.

When you risk telling someone the truth about yourself, you are vulnerable, and vulnerability is scary. The faith in yourself to move through the fear will grow over time, as you risk being your true self out loud and build love for yourself and between you and others.

Embracing Grief

One hard thing about being human is to embrace the paradox that while you have agency and can influence others and your environment, you cannot control others or the world around you. You are empowered and are also a humble being who cannot know how your life will unfold and cannot bend the world to suit you. You don't know for sure how this moment will affect the events to come and so cannot say with certainty what is good and what is bad. For many, facing the truth of not knowing can feel worrisome and painful. Having practice and trust in your ability to protect yourself can make the inevitable slings and arrows of outrageous fortune hit less hard.

We often tell ourselves stories about what we need to make sure bad things don't happen. To make sure you don't face the grief of not getting what you want in your marriage, you don't say what you are hoping for.

Resentment and disappointment build up instead. To make sure a friend-ship doesn't end, you don't speak up when something painful is happening. You hide your true feelings, maybe even from yourself. To make sure your child doesn't feel badly, you flex your boundaries and buy candy or new toys, even though you said you wouldn't and can't afford to. Many times, if you choose not to act within your integrity—to speak authentically or set a needed boundary—what you are doing is avoiding grief.

There are many kinds of grief you can try to avoid by not doing internal and external boundary work. You might avoid witnessing a hard feeling in another. You can avoid ending a relationship and the pain that will come as you let it go. You can avoid the fear of being left. You might avoid the grief of facing past hardships or processing traumas.

We do a lot to avoid grief. Many of us are taught that grief is bad. But grief is not bad. Grief is helpful; grief is a gift.

When I think about grief, I always think about love. I believe that love is the word we use to describe our own felt-sense recognition of the vast value of someone or something. When I say, "I love my daughter," what does that mean? It means I see her vast worth and connect to that vast worth. I feel her immense value as an embodied cellular knowing: the emotion we have named *love*. When we see another person and celebrate their value, the word we use for seeing and feeling the truth of their worth is love.

Without love, we would not have grief. Love is the felt-sense acknowl-edgment of the value of a being; grief holds full awareness that something hard or harsh has happened to that being. Grief can be a measure of how much we love and have loved both others and ourselves. If you want to face reality in all of its impermanence, all of its harshness, and all of its beauty, then you must hold love and grief simultaneously. It is impossible to hold deep awareness of love without also holding deep awareness of loss. And so, when we love deeply, we hold both love and grief inextricably intertwined.

Many times, you might avoid speaking up about what is not okay for you because of fear that it might cause a permanent shift in your relation-ship with another person. Maybe that shift could even lead to the end of an important relationship. The grief we face when these shifts happen can be huge. If you don't acknowledge that you might make a request and have it go unmet—or that you might make a boundary that leads to a rupture—then you will likely inadvertently avoid setting boundaries and making requests, so as not to face these hard feelings. But life can be more fulfilling and feel more whole and worth living when you don't avoid communicating what's true for you to the people you care about.

Do you know how you feel about grief? Think of grief as the act of facing loss. It could mean loss of something or someone close to you, such as through a death, a breakup, or job loss. Grief is also the process you go through when you face the loss of a hope for how things would go. This type of grief is usually called "disappointment." Some moments of disappointment feel huge and other less so. "Regret" is another word that we use to describe grief. Regret is when you feel grief about your own actions in the past. Perhaps the actions cost you something in the form of direct consequences, or perhaps you were out of your integrity or hurt someone else. Exploring your relationship with grief will support you in embracing boundary work rather than avoiding it.

An invitation to explore: Take some time to explore your relationship with grief, large and small. Use these prompts:

- *When I was growing up, the messages I got about grief (out loud or implied) were...*

- *When I was growing up, my parents responded to moments I was grieving or disappointed by...*

- *When I was growing up, each family member responded to their own grief or disappointment by...*

- *When someone I know is going through a loss, I usually...*

- *If I make a request of a friend, and they say no, I usually feel...*

- *If I make a request of my partner, and they say no, I usually feel...*

- *If I feel regret about actions of mine in the past, I usually…*

- *Right now, when I think about grief in others, I feel…*

- *Right now, when I think about grief in myself, I feel…*

Setting a boundary will likely have at least small moments of grief. If you have trouble setting boundaries that stick, you might be trying to avoid grief and disappointment by collapsing your boundaries. You might tell yourself a story that it's bad when the other person feels sadness or agitation as they face the loss of not having things go as they were expecting. You can help yourself with this by revisiting the listening with acceptance part of the psychological boundary. Keep your psychological boundary in between the two of you, so you can bear witness kindly to the loss the other person is processing. Just be there with them, with compassion. You don't have to do anything else.

Rather than flexing your external boundary to soothe someone else, hold both your boundary and the reality of their difficult feelings at once. It is not your job to change their feelings, because their feelings are functional and have a purpose, and all feelings are welcome. Practice listening with acceptance of their feelings while you hold onto your boundaries. That way, you love yourself and the other person at the same time.

If you do end up setting a boundary that leads to an outcome that brings grief, see that as an invitation from your heart to hold both vast value and love and a hard reality at the same time. As you do, you might find yourself changed on the other side of that emotional journey. It may be that change leads to new paths and ways of being that you cannot yet imagine. Emotions help you shift through time, and this emergent process leads you to new ways of experiencing the world.

Whether or not you choose to set a boundary, you might have to face some aspect of grief. If you don't align your behavior with what is and is not okay for you, then you'll have to deal with the grief of not standing up for yourself, or grieve having an external reality in which standing up for yourself is threatening to you in some way. If you do not follow through on your boundaries, you may have to experience the grief of not aligning with your integrity, or the grief that the world is not safe enough for you to exist freely in it. If you do set and follow through on an external boundary, then you might have to face and process temporary, partial, or even full rupture in a relationship. There's grief, no matter what. Ugh! That's a hard reality. Before you shy away, however, remember that boundaries are an act of love and kindness for others as well as for yourself.

One of the things I feel great grief about is the inequality in our society, and how people experience their safety and threat level differently every day because of oppression. There are folks whom our society attacks and marginalizes relentlessly. As a cisgender white woman, it is easier and safer for me to set boundaries than it is for many with different lived experiences. I am determined to use my privilege and skills to be a small part of changing those conditions, and the grief I feel about oppression spurs me forward to work harder. Grief often does that—it gives us reasons to move forward to create something with purpose and meaning.

My culture calls lots of things wrong that are just wonderful ways of showing up human. I want you to use your boundaries to uphold and uplift your beautiful humanness, not to let anyone else define what your boundaries should be. I also trust you to set boundaries when it okay to do so, and I face the grief with you that, depending on your circumstances, many times it is not safe enough to use your voice.

Soft Front, Strong Back, Wild Heart

When it comes to living a life that is connected, compassionate, authentic, and kind, the best quick guide I have found comes from combining the thoughts of Joan Halifax (2021) and Brene Brown (2020) in the phrase: "soft front, strong back, wild heart." Inner boundary work and external boundary work are some of the tools you can use to make it more possible to live with a soft front, strong back, and wild heart.

Soft front means leading with vulnerability and compassion while sharing more of yourself when it feels right and helpful. It means speaking without an armor of defensiveness or guardedness. This does not mean sharing everything you are thinking and feeling all the time. I support your discernment about who has shown you that they can hold intimacy with you well. If you must armor up to be in certain situations or even to live most days of your life because of oppression, I respect this and support you, as well. If you've had trouble finding places to have a soft, open front, I encourage you to seek out safe friends and community spaces, identity-based affinity groups, and healing circles where you can experience a more open vulnerability because the environment is safer.

Showing up with compassion and curiosity and respect for common humanity as your guide does not mean that you need others to change themselves. Your psychological boundary will help you add protection so that you can be in your soft front. The soft front stance helps us remember, with humility, the reality of our limited human vision: we can rest in the knowledge that we do not know everything. This resting into not knowing supports deeper listening and curiosity so that when you listen to others you will listen to understand rather than listen to defend or support your next point. To lead with this much vulnerability, you will need a strong back made up of boundaries you can count on.

Strong back means you can trust yourself to protect yourself. You trust yourself to make moves to increase your safety and well-being when things are happening that are not okay. You trust yourself to make those complex and nuanced decisions as you face a world that is not in your control, a world that might be hurting you, where the answer you are looking for has no easy or right solution. You build trust in yourself to listen to the wisdom inside you to define for yourself what feels okay and does not feel okay. You trust yourself not to take in others' thoughts and feelings about you as wholly true, but instead you discern and take in only the feedback that helps you to grow and connect.

Having a strong back means you trust yourself to pause and align your actions with your integrity, and you protect yourself enough to be able to lean into challenging conversations. You are able to share yourself in ways that are thoughtful and kind, though maybe not what is considered "nice" to many. When I think of stereotypical niceness, I think about showing up in a way that anticipates the feelings of others and tries to manage them by hiding some of your truth and feelings. This kind of nice means that you do not trust others to handle their own feelings or your truth and you don't trust your relationships to handle hard moments or to connect through differences. In contrast, we can strive to be kind. Kindness means I trust you enough to share my reality with you even if you don't like it. Kindness comes when you trust in your own boundary building enough to risk approaching the world with a soft front of curiosity and compassion rather than with hard armor, because you know you will protect yourself when needed.

If you are not all the way there in trusting your boundary work, that is normal. You are practicing, and practice will change your brain. Every time you try to work these boundaries, you trust yourself more to treat yourself well. Keep working to build the strong back you need to support your authenticity.

If you add the soft front and strong back to the stance of *wild heart*, you will add your commitment to your own authenticity. You have to be in a close enough relationship with yourself to hear your authentic voice. You may have to find some time to be within yourself and away from other people's voices and cries for help to hear it, but I promise it is there. Your wild heart will tell you things about yourself and show you the differences you have from others. Some might push you away when they hear your truth. It might be that your authenticity leads to risk taking in your career or relationships or has messages for you about big changes to make in how you show up in the world. These may bring you joy as well as grief.

In our current Western culture, power is often seen as finite and, because of this, as something to be hoarded and protected. I believe this hurts all of us, and especially those who are lower on the power hierarchy ladders that we have built. There is another way to think about power: power as abundant, shareable, and increasable. This is power-with thinking rather than power-over thinking. In this mindset, the more I empower you, the more things go well for all of us. In this way of thinking, there is no ladder.

Each one of the tools you have learned in this book are about supporting a power-with way of being. When I accept your feelings and have the psychological safety to believe you without losing myself (psychological boundaries), I empower you to share more of yourself. When I am thoughtful about how my behavior affects our relationship, I honor my power to influence the situation (containing boundaries). When I honor my personal needs for safety, given my history, preferences, identity, and social location, I empower me to protect myself as best as possible (physical boundaries). When I use all of this to share with others what feels good for me and not good for me, without trying to control them, I honor our mutual empowerment (external boundaries). You can use these tools to live in a power-with way. It will empower others while empowering you too.

It takes bravery to live guided by your wild heart, especially if you are committed to doing it without armoring up on the front end. With some boundaries to assist with your self-protection, a ton of self-compassion, and some patience around this being a journey and a process, I trust that you can do it.

Acknowledgments

Wow, you are still reading this book, thank you! Thanks for taking in these ideas and trying them on and supporting yourself in your boundary work. I am so grateful to you for being part of this ride with me.

My greatest teachers have always been those clients and students who share their humanity with me in my therapy and teaching spaces. I have learned more from you all about how complexity works, how emergence happens, how love and grief heal, and how true hope works than I could ever learn from any book. To my clients: I am grateful and honored to have worked with you, to have walked with you, and to have learned from you. To those who have studied with me, thank you for pushing me, for challenging me, for asking me to grow with you. Special thanks to Ran, Kelly, Jami Lynn, Rebecca, Jen, Sara, and Kim. Your presence has meant everything to me for all these years I have been growing this work. I cannot thank you enough for showing up with me again and again.

Of all my teachers, two stand out particularly when it comes to this text. One, who is my guide in all that I do in my work as a therapist and a teacher, is Bonnie Badenoch. Thank you for being a mentor; thank you for walking the path as truly as you talk about it. Your actions and way of being are as much an inspiration to me as your teachings, and I am forever grateful that you are part of my life. I also owe enormous thanks to one of my early mentors, Carol Middelberg. It was with her guidance and ideas that the six steps began to take seed in my brain, and it is out of conversations with her that my boundary work with myself and with my clients began in earnest. Thank you for your early guidance and for being a great mentor when I needed to be challenged and guided simultaneously. You have an art for interweaving the two, and that was like magic for me. Special thanks to Kim May, my friend, your boundaries are so delightfully good that being with you has made all of my boundaries better. Your modeling has given me hope and inspiration.

None of the way I think or share this work could be possible without the writings and teachings of some of the wonderful thinkers, philosophers, and scientists of our times, some of whom I have studied with through their writings and lectures. I am grateful to David Eagleman, bell hooks, Jaak Panksepp, Maya Angelou, Alice Walker, Jim Collins, Bill Lazier, Sonya Renee Taylor, Iain McGilchrist, Emily Dickinson, Antonio Damasio, Ijeoma Oluo, Robert Sapolsky, Tyson Yunkaporta, Robin Wall Kimmerer, Edith Eger, Brené Brown, Angus Fletcher, Lucille Clifton, Richard Rohr, Emily Nagoski, Lisa Feldman Barrett, Austin Channing Brown, Joan Halifax, Tarana Burke, and Mary Oliver. Others I have been fortunate enough to study with personally, including Ed Tronick, Dan Siegel, Richard Schwartz, Maggie Kline, Peter Levine, Stephen Porges, Bruce Ecker, and Sunny Lansdale. Thank you all for the work you do and for the wisdom you share. You have changed me in all the ways that matter.

Thanks to Jennye Garibaldi and the folks at New Harbinger for seeing a book in these ideas when I was first fleshing them out and for sticking with me through my process as a first-time writer. Your belief in this work helped me see it might be helpful to others. I am so grateful for our partnership.

Writing is truly a group endeavor, and I thank all my readers, friends, and supporters, especially Abe Louise Young. You saw what I was trying to say and helped me make it readable and clear. Truly, the book would not be in this form without you, and I have no words to express my trust in you and my gratitude. To Akilah Riley-Richardson, your clarity and guidance are always spot on, and without you, this text would not reach many who I am hoping to walk with and learn from. Thank you a thousand times for lending your wisdom.

I also want to thank Maneena Douglas and Ann Stoneson. Maneena— you are such a wonderful friend, a guiding light for me in gentleness and thoughtfulness and sensitivity. Thank you for holding me through this process—it meant the world to me. Ann, my therapy wife, my dear friend, you are a guide to me in your presence and the way you honor your needs and body and heart while holding others in your heart too. You not only have helped me and inspired me as I took on this project but have helped me every step of the way these last ten years. I am forever grateful for our friendship.

Most of all, I want to thank my family, Adam and Stella. You have stuck with me through countless hours when it would have been way more helpful and fun for me to be cooking, playing, or being, but I was writing. You have supported me through all my worries, stresses, and freak-outs. Stella, you are an inspiration to me, and I hope that this book is part of making a more respectful and kinder world for you. Thank you for being yourself and teaching me all about the art of being human. You are my star. Adam, my love, none of this work would be possible without you. You are steady and fierce in your support of me, of the work, of our family, and I do not have words big enough to tell you how thankful I am that we said yes to each other on that altar all those years ago. Thank you for all you have said and done to make our life possible. I love you.

References

Badenoch, B. 2018. *Heart of Trauma: Healing the Embodied Brain in the Context of Relationships*. New York: W. W. Norton.

Barrett, L. F. 2017. *How Emotions Are Made: The Secret Life of the Brain*. New York: Houghton Mifflin Harcourt.

Brown, B. 2011. "Shame, Perfectionism and Embracing Wholehearted Living." *Iris* 61: 12–16.

———. 2017. *Braving the Wilderness: The Quest for True Belonging and the Courage to Stand Alone*. New York: Penguin Random House.

———. 2020. "Strong Backs, Soft Fronts, and Wild Hearts." *Unlocking Us* podcast, November 4. https://brenebrown.com/podcast/brene-on-strong-backs-soft-fronts-and-wild-hearts.

Damasio, A. 1994. *Descartes' Error: Emotion, Reason, and the Human Brain*. New York: Penguin Press.

———. 2021. *Feeling and Knowing: Making Minds Conscious*. New York: Pantheon Press.

Dennis-Tiwary, T. 2022. *Future Tense: Why Anxiety Is Good for You (Even Though It Feels Bad)*. New York: HarperCollins.

Eagleman, D. 2021. *Livewired: The Inside Story of the Ever-Changing Brain*. New York: Vintage Books.

Ecker, B., R. Ticic, and L. Hulley. 2012. *Unlocking the Emotional Brain: Eliminating Symptoms at Their Roots Using Memory Reconsolidation*. New York: Routledge.

Gu, S., W. Wang, F. Wang, and J. H. Huang. 2016. "Neuromodulator and Emotion Biomarker for Stress Induced Mental Disorders." *Neural Plasticity* 2016: 2609128.

Halifax, J. 2021. "Strong Back, Soft Front." *Dropping In*, an Omega podcast curated by Cali Alpert, January 19. https://www.eomega.org/audio/strong-back-soft-front.

Imms, P., J. F. Domínguez, D. A. Burmester, C. Seguin, A. Clemente, T. Dhollander, P. H. Wilson, G. Poudel, and K. Caeyenberghs. 2021. "Navigating the Link Between Processing Speed and Network Communication in the Human Brain." *Brain Structure and Function* 226(4): 1281–1302.

Johansson, C., and A. Lansner. 2007. "Imposing Biological Constraints onto an Abstract Neocortical Attractor Network Model." *Neural Computation* 19(7): 1871–96.

Kahneman, D. 2011. *Thinking, Fast and Slow*. New York: Farrar, Straus, and Giroux.

Kandel, E. 2006. *In Search of Memory: The Emergence of a New Science of Mind*. New York: W. W. Norton.

Levine, P. A. 2015. *Trauma and Memory: Brain and Body in a Search for the Living Past*. Berkeley, CA: North Atlantic Books.

Longe, O., F. A. Maratos, P. Gilbert, G. Evans, F. Volker, H. Rockliff, and G. Rippon. 2010. "Having a Word with Yourself: Neural Correlates of Self-Criticism and Self-Reassurance." *Neuroimage* 49(2): 1849–56.

Luyten, P., and P. Fonagy. 2015. "The Neurobiology of Mentalizing." *Personality Disorders: Theory, Research, and Treatment* 6(4): 366–79.

McGilchrist, I. 2009. *The Master and His Emissary: The Divided Brain and the Making of the Western World*. New Haven, CT: Yale University Press.

Menakem, R. 2017. *My Grandmother's Hands: Racialized Trauma and the Pathway to Mending Our Hearts and Bodies*. Las Vegas: Central Recovery Press.

Murthy, V. H. 2020. *Together: The Healing Power of Human Connection in a Sometimes Lonely World*. New York: HarperCollins.

Muscatell, K. A., S. A. Morelli, E. B. Falk, B. M. Way, J. H. Pfeifer, A. D. Galinsky, M. D. Lieberman, M. Dapretto, and N. I. Eisenberger. 2012. "Social Status Modulates Neural Activity in the Mentalizing Network." *NeuroImage* 60(3): 1771–77.

Neff, K. 2011. *Self-Compassion: Stop Beating Yourself Up and Leave Insecurity Behind*. New York: William Morrow.

Overwalle, F. V., and M. Vandekerckhove. 2013. "Implicit and Explicit Social Mentalizing: Dual Processes Driven by a Shared Neural Network." *Frontiers in Human Neuroscience* 7: 560.

Panksepp, J., and L. Biven. 2012. *The Archaeology of Mind: Neuroevolutionary Origins of Human Emotion*. New York: W. W. Norton.

Porges, S. W. 2011. *The Polyvagal Theory: Neurophysiological Foundations of Emotions, Attachment, Communication, and Self-Regulation*. New York: W. W. Norton.

Sapolsky, R. M. 2017. *Behave: The Biology of Humans at Our Best and Worst*. New York: Penguin Press.

Siegel, D. J. 2010a. *Mindsight: The New Science of Personal Transformation*. New York: Bantam Books.

———. 2010b. *The Mindful Therapist: A Clinician's Guide to Mindsight and Neural Integration*. New York: W. W. Norton.

———. 2020. *The Developing Mind: How Relationships and the Brain Interact to Shape Who We Are*, 3rd ed. New York: Guilford Press.

Stevens, L., M. Gauthier-Braham, and B. Bush. 2018. "The Brain That Longs to Care for Itself: The Current Neuroscience of Self-Compassion." In *The Neuroscience of Empathy, Compassion, and Self-Compassion*, edited by L. Stevens and C. C. Woodruff. Cambridge, MA: Elsevier Academic Press.

Tronick, E., and C. M. Gold. 2020. *The Power of Discord: Why the Ups and Downs of Relationships Are the Secret to Building Intimacy, Resilience, and Trust*. New York: Little, Brown Spark.

Yordanova, Y. N., H. Duffau, and G. Herbet. 2017. "Neural Pathways Subserving Face-Based Mentalizing." *Brain Structure and Function* 222(7): 3087–3105.

Juliane Taylor Shore, LMFT, is a clinician, storyteller, and teacher of interpersonal neurobiology who lives with her husband, daughter, and dog in the hill country on the outskirts of Austin, TX. Shore specializes in trauma recovery and relational healing for individual adults and romantic partnerships, and also spends much of her time teaching therapists internationally. When she is not working, she is usually playing with her family, reading poetry, and making random art projects for fun.

Foreword writer Rebecca Wong, LCSW-R, is a trauma therapist and educator who specializes in integrative somatic modalities for relational trauma resolution. She's on a quest to help folks heal the legacy of transgenerational trauma, increase trust in the wisdom of their protective systems, and develop Connectfulness® practices that support relational wellness for generations to come.

Real change *is* possible

For more than forty-five years, New Harbinger has
published proven-effective self-help books and pioneering
workbooks to help readers of all ages and backgrounds
improve mental health and well-being, and achieve lasting
personal growth. In addition, our spirituality books
offer profound guidance for deepening awareness and
cultivating healing, self-discovery, and fulfillment.

Founded by psychologist Matthew McKay and Patrick
Fanning, New Harbinger is proud to be an independent,
employee-owned company. Our books reflect our
core values of integrity, innovation, commitment,
sustainability, compassion, and trust. Written by leaders
in the field and recommended by therapists worldwide,
New Harbinger books are practical, accessible, and
provide real tools for real change.

newharbingerpublications

MORE BOOKS from
NEW HARBINGER PUBLICATIONS

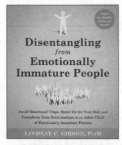